KIERKEGAARD
An Introduction

KIERKEGAARD

An Introduction

BY HERMANN DIEM

translated by David Green

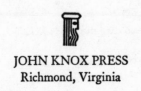

JOHN KNOX PRESS
Richmond, Virginia

Translated from the German with the approval of Verlag Vandenhoeck & Ruprecht. German title — *Sören Kierkegaard: Eine Einführung.*

Scripture quotations are from the *Revised Standard Version of the Bible,* copyrighted 1946 and 1952.

LIBRARY OF CONGRESS CATALOG CARD NUMBER: 66-17278

© M. E. BRATCHER 1966

PRINTED IN THE UNITED STATES OF AMERICA

J. 3555 (W. B.) 262

Contents

Kierkegaard and His Century

It is quite possible to study the theological and intellectual history of the nineteenth century without noticing that during the first half of the century—from 1813 to 1855—in the rather remote city of Copenhagen, there lived a remarkable man: Søren Kierkegaard. In his own country he did cause considerable disturbance for a while, but it subsided soon after his death and word of it scarcely penetrated beyond Denmark at the time. A few rather small groups of sectarians and other outsiders kept his memory alive for a while. The officials of the church, the state, and the business community, however, could make nothing of him.

Kierkegaard was of no significance for the intellectual history of the nineteenth century. All the problems of our century, in contrast, have gathered around his work, meeting there as at a focal point; we see our problems better in Kierkegaard than almost anywhere else. As an immediate illustration, let us consider one of the most important points at which we today are still deeply sensitive to these problems: Kierkegaard's dispute with the philosophy of Hegel.

The significance of Hegelian philosophy and the problems it raises confront us today primarily in the way it has been applied and developed by Marxism. Even if philosophic discussion of Hegel's system of pure thought were long since closed, even if its impossibility had been demonstrated, nothing could alter the fact that in Marxism we are dealing with a potent political and social force whose ideology derives from Hegel's philosophy and possesses an extremely aggressive vitality. When Kierkegaard took the field against Hegel, he knew nothing as yet of Karl Marx. Neither did he concern himself with Hegel's philosophy of the state. He began instead by attacking the logical basis of the Hegelian system. He was concerned with the concept of reality, the great problem with which Kant's critique of reason had confronted philosophy. Retreat to the pre-Kantian status was impossible. Hegel made a magnificent attempt to combine thought and being in a system of pure thought in which the absolute thinks of itself in one's thinking of the absolute. Kierkegaard looked on this attempt as basically dishonest, disingenuous, a fraud he never tired of exposing. In this fashion, with the aid of thought, Hegel sought to comprehend and establish reality; but this reality was and would remain a purely noumenal reality, moving in the medium of abstraction. The subject doing this pure thinking could be only a divine being capable of surveying all the history of the world and of mankind, not a human being living himself within this history and reflecting on his own life within this history.

Despite all his efforts, therefore, Hegel could not demonstrate the crucial point: how I, an empirical thinker, am to transform myself into this absolute subject thinking pure thought and thus become "theocentric." Kierkegaard liked to compare Hegel to a man who has built a magnificent palace but cannot live in it himself, and makes the gatehouse his home. The greatness of the Hegelian conception struck a responsive chord in Kierkegaard. It is probably safe to say that he would not have attacked it so passionately had it not represented for himself an extremely dangerous temptation. But once he had recognized that Hegel could set his dialectic in motion and keep it only with the help of a fraud, he had to resist this temptation bravely. Hegel had avoided the issue to some extent at the crucial point, a fact which Kierkegaard considered not merely a formal intellectual error, but nothing less than an act of dishonesty. The issue that Hegel avoided is the existence of the thinker himself. The reality that he missed, for which he substituted the fantastic pseudo-reality of pure thought, is the reality of the thinker who himself exists, who contemplates his own existence in order to exist in reality.

The categories by which Kierkegaard judged Hegel were therefore all ethical categories. Of course this did not mean that he would carry on his dispute with Hegel in the passion of moral indignation. He carried it on instead with the most reasoned and subtle inquiries into the relationship between logic and ontology, but at the same time with all the considerable powers of irony and humor at his disposal. He reproached Hegel for being without humor. He considered this argument every bit as central and weighty as his objections to Hegel's logic; for, he said, "whoever seeks to show himself an authority in the intellectual world today must above all else have a sense of humor." Everything that Kierkegaard says against Hegel is grounded in the ethical passion of the thinking man infinitely interested in his own existence. Existing in this way, he does not reflect *on* the truth of reality; he is *in* truth, because he *exists* in reality.

Kierkegaard saw that we are dealing here with an ethical question, that is, the question of how a man ought to shape his existence. With this insight he anticipated the criticism that Karl Marx was later to make of Hegel. He saw that what Hegel calls "spirit" can easily be replaced by "nature." Then the "idea," which, according to Hegel, controls the movement of history, simply becomes the immanent organizing principle of nature. The course of history becomes a natural process. But this development leaves no room for the individual existing man responsible for his own decisions. The individual takes his place in history by joining in this natural process and becoming one with it. This is precisely the idea that Karl Marx used as his point of departure in order, as he put it, to stand Hegel's philosophy on its head, turning Hegel's idealism into historical materialism.

What is more, Kierkegaard also predicted the political consequences of this development. As early as 1846, he wrote a critique of the contemporary social and political situation in which he predicted with remarkable accuracy not only the events of 1848 but also the course of political and social development down to the present day. It should be stated in advance that he was personally as conservative as a man could possibly be, and inveighed against even the slightest concession to the liberal tendencies of his period, both in politics and in the church. He took it most amiss that Bishop Mynster of Seeland ordained the leader of the liberals. Even his king was not conservative enough for his taste. At the same time, however, he saw that the leveling of all authorities and concrete restrictions could no longer be delayed, and that the authorities in power were responsible for this state of affairs. Two years before the Revolution of 1848, he wrote:

> If authority and power have once been misused in the world and brought upon themselves the nemesis of revolution, it is because they really were impotence and weakness trying to stand on their own feet, thereby bringing this nemesis upon themselves.

The people in power have surrendered their own authority, which they can no longer restore by a return to earlier political systems. In a country as strongly Lutheran as Denmark, it would have been logical to use divine authority to support the exising powers and ordinances; such authority is part of the Lutheran theory of the state. The possibility of doing so never entered Kierkegaard's head. In this situation all theories of the state and fundamental justifications of its power lose their relevance. Only one concern remains: to find new points of departure in a world that is already falling apart. Nor could Kierkegaard share his period's general antipathy toward the proletariat, which was about to mount the stage of world politics. He recalled instead the disgraceful role played by the "common man" in "Christian" society and declared that the church had itself given birth to the proletariat, or at least contributed to its formation.

> The thing that is un-Christian and immoral is to base the state on a foundation of men whom one ignores, whose kinship one denies—even while preaching a moving Sunday sermon about love of one's neighbor.

In this situation, there is one special danger to avoid: one must not prevent the existing order from being called in question by defending it on *false* grounds. What is all-important is to be conservative in the *right* way, as Kierkegaard was and sought to be. Under these circumstances, any attempt to defend the existing order at all costs and reject everything that calls it in question issues a challenge to just the wrong kind of change, like that represented by the progressive political movements. Individual personal responsibility no longer propels the movement; instead, the individuals converge in a mass in order to share in the progress of the species. It was obvious to Kierkegaard that this course, taken by the Socialist or Communist movement, provides no answer.

> There is no chance that the idea of socialism and community will become the salvation of our age. What will save us is rather the accompanying skepticism, which will allow the development to proceed correctly. Every individual will either be lost or, caught up in abstractions, win back his own self.

He saw the course of development as follows:

> In our age, the principle of association (which can be valid at best only

in respect to material things) is not affirmative, but negative. It is an escape, a distraction, a mirage. Its dialectic is to strengthen individuals and thereby enervate them. It strengthens through the numerical power of union; but such strength is ethical weakness. When the single individual has achieved an ethical stance in the face of the entire world, only then does true union become possible. Otherwise the union of individually weak men is a thing just as ugly and pernicious as the marriage of children.

The leveling process of socialism cannot, however, be brought to a halt by any attempt to make the wheel of history turn backward. The important thing is to be on the lookout for future possibilities—that is, to ask what must happen when the individuals begin once more to emerge from this leveling process. Here is Kierkegaard's vision of this pathway to the future:

> The species has itself sought leveling and emancipation; it has willed the destruction of authority and at the same time its own destruction. Once it has kindled the cheerless blaze of abstraction in the skepticism of Socialism; once it has used the skepticism of Socialism to level out all individuality and all concrete organic reality, achieving instead "mankind" and quantitative equality between one man and the next; once it has thus delighted for a moment in the broad expanse of infinity, unbroken by any limiting prominence, not even the slightest, but consisting entirely of "empty air and water"—once this happens, then the work can begin, since the individuals must help themselves, every man for himself.

Only in this fashion can the leveling process be overcome productively by those individuals that have worked their way through it, all the while shaping a new criterion of greatness and precedence. Only thus can the failure of the fallen authorities be made good, a failure which, according to Kierkegaard, consists in "neglect of the religious uniqueness of the individual before God and of responsibility to the standards of eternity."

This is the future course of events as Kierkegaard saw it. Should he summon up all the force of his conservatism to try to stem the tide, knowing that this course of events threatens an immense loss of concrete obligations, with all their inestimable benefits for the ethical training and cultural development of human beings? Or should he instead support and thereby hasten the inescapable future, knowing that the leveling process can ultimately be arrested only when, as he put it, "the individual in his individual uniqueness achieves the confidence of religiosity"? Kierkegaard could do neither; he justified his position with a statement that hints at the violent tensions, both personal and material, involved in the task he set out to perform. "The leveling process must run its course," he said; nevertheless, "it must come as offense must come into the world, but woe to him by whom it comes."

Now in spite of these eminently political views, Kierkegaard remained aloof from all political talk and action. A greater contrast is scarcely conceivable than that between the public world in which political decisions are reached and debated and the way of life of an independent scholar like Kierkegaard, who writes books about the most esoteric aesthetic, philosophic, and religious subjects while leading the life of a well-to-do crank who apparently feels neither the need nor the desire to assume any public office or responsibility. On occasion he became the subject of public discussion; his name appeared in the newspapers. This seemed in part due to his gaucherie and in part a typical example of journalistic sensationalism. He had refused to tolerate praise given him by the *Corsair,* a vicious satirical paper published in Copenhagen; it retaliated by making such a fool of him that for a long time he was the laughingstock of all the Copenhagen guttersnipes. No one suspected that he had deliberately provoked this attack with two purposes in mind: first, to expose the vulgarity of this kind of press; but at the same time also to demonstrate the worthlessness of a population that supports such a press. Finally, at the end of his life, he emerged from the seclusion of his life as a writer and loosed a shockingly violent attack upon the church in newspaper articles and pamphlets, an attack that culminated in the accusation that the church was living off a Christianity that had long since vanished, and that the clergy were "cannibals," cannibals "of the most loathsome sort." But even this attack seemed to be an internal controversy within the church, irrelevant to the world of politics —the more so because Kierkegaard would have nothing to do with any interference, not to mention support, on the part of political movements.

But let us recall once more what he considered to be the mortal danger threatened by the course of political events and the only possible means of escape. The political powers and authorities have corrupted themselves. The existing order has brought upon itself the avenging nemesis of revolution against all present class distinctions, differences of rank, and social obligations. Once underway, the leveling process cannot be arrested. The only way of escape lies ahead, the hope that the isolated individual will once more work his way out of this process in order to achieve the confidence of religiosity through a sense of uniqueness and responsibility before God—otherwise he will perish. But this way to deliverance cannot be opened by any political movement, nor indeed by any movement directed at the mob. One must rather turn to the individual, one must do everything in one's power to fragment the mass into individuals—this course of action, and it alone, is political in the deepest sense.

Here Kierkegaard found his great example in Socrates:

> "The individual"—this category has achieved final dialectical validity only once, at the very outset, in Socrates, who brought about the dissolution of the pagan world. Its function in Christendom will be the exact opposite: it will serve a second time to turn men (Christians) into Christians. We are not dealing here with the category to be employed by the missionary that preaches Christianity to pagans, but with the category that must be used within Christendom itself by the missionary that must introduce Christianity into Christendom.

Kierkegaard sees himself confronted with the task of introducing Christianity into Christendom, even though he lives in what is still a homogeneous "Christian" society. What we today call Western Christian civilization, for the defense and preservation of which we labor, stood secure, at least on the surface. Church and state were intimately united in a mutual guarantee. The religious devotion and education of the period had achieved a happy synthesis in its best representatives.

Admittedly, this christianized world no longer went unchallenged. We have already seen that political liberalism and Socialism were knocking loudly at the doors of states still ruled in the spirit of the "Holy Alliance." They also posed a threat to the church, whose institutions and privileges were bound up in the state. But the challenge went even deeper. Behind these political movements stood a science that was about to emancipate itself completely from the Christian faith, especially the modern natural sciences and the science of history. Here, too, Kierkegaard was far ahead of his contemporaries in his insight into the imminent dangers. While his century was still enjoying the enthusiasm of discovery brought about by the progress of the mechanistic philosophy of the natural sciences, he said:

> Most of what presently flourishes vigorously under the name of science (especially the natural sciences) is not science at all, but curiosity. — Ultimate ruin will finally come from the natural sciences.

He mounted his strongest attack against materialistic physiology with its methodology of dissection and microscopic examination, an approach that makes it impossible to treat man as a spiritual being. "What Satan can endure this!" He saw the same materialistic education at work in the historical school that is interested only in reconstructing the events of the past without allowing man any relationship to this past history.

> The spirit lives in two questions: first, is what has been said possible? and second, can I do it? But two other questions betray the absence of the spirit: first, is it really true? and second, has my neighbor Christophersen done it, has he really done it?

Here, too, he was already attacking the errors and crudities of historicism, errors that the intellectual world has become aware of only gradually in our century. This holds particularly for the effects of the historical approach upon theology, which has been increasingly embarrassed by historical investigation into the life of Jesus and in fact quite generally by the historical-critical study of the Bible. For a long time the theologians tried to fight a delaying action against historical-critical investigation and to base faith and theology upon the results of historical study. Kierkegaard, in contrast, had this to say:

> What a stroke of luck it is that this hopeful hypothesis, the dearest wish of critical theology, is an impossibility, because even its most complete realization will still be only an approximation. And again, what a stroke of luck for the men of science that the error is by no means theirs! Were all the angels to join forces they could still produce only an approximation, because, for historical knowledge, approximation is the only certainty—but it is still not enough to provide a basis for eternal bliss. Now I will assume the contrary: the enemy has succeeded in proving what he likes about the Scripture, with such certainty that it exceeds the fondest dream of the most bitter enemy. Now what? Has the enemy now done away with Christianity? Hardly. Has he harmed the faith? No, not in the least. Has he won the right to disclaim responsibility if

he is not a believer? Not at all. Just because these books were not written by these authors, are not authentic, not integral, not inspired (inspiration, however, cannot be disproven, since it is an object of faith), it does not follow that these authors never lived, and especially that Christ never lived. It still remains just as easy for the believer to make these assumptions, note, just as easy; for, were he to make these assumptions on the strength of a proof, he would be on the point of losing his faith . . . Why then is proof offered? Faith does not need it, must even consider it an enemy. If, however, faith begins to be ashamed of itself; if, like a woman dissatisfied with her love, who is secretly ashamed of the man she loves and so demands proof that he is exceptional, faith begins to lose its passion; if, in other words, faith begins to cease to be faith, then proof becomes necessary so that the man who has lost his faith may still enjoy the approbation of the bourgeois. On this point, many clergymen misled by a confusion of categories expound rhetorical nonsense—but this we shall not even discuss.

Kierkegaard was not in the least afraid of all these phenomena challenging Christianity, as his contemporaries were. The challenges only enabled him to define the true nature of Christianity all the more clearly and unassailably. What he was afraid of, though, and resisted passionately, was the attempt to pretend that the challenge was not real and to act as though all were well with Christianity. Here once more he ran up against his great antagonist Hegel. Hegel's philosophy had enabled Christianity to escape the challenge of the phenomena that should have disturbed it most deeply. What is more, it was even possible to see this development as a necessary stage in the historical process in which the idea realizes itself. Hegelian philosophy had transcended all opposites by means of a higher unity and even defined the Christian faith as a stage in the historical process by which the spirit develops and comes back to itself. The theologians brought up on Hegel perfected the speculative theory of this happy synthesis between philosophy and Christianity, between reason and revelation. Christendom as a whole—with or without this theological and philosophical foundation—realized the synthesis in practice through a way of life in which education and the practice of religion, the struggle for worldly goods and the Christian faith, were united in unquestioned harmony.

Such prosperity of worldly Christendom could only pose an enormous dilemma to real Christianity. In Kierkegaard's opinion, it was hardly

possible any longer to gain a decisive impression of the Christian faith
from within Christendom as it actually was. Christianity had won a
Pyrrhic victory by entering the "Christian" world and being absorbed
by it. By making Christianity a topic for speculative, historical, or
aesthetic study instead of a concern affecting the existence of every
individual, the philosophers swindled the world and robbed it of Christianity. At the same time, they also corrupted humanity; for humanity
can be healthy only when each man is passionately concerned with the
way he should live his life. For Kierkegaard it was crucial that these
two, human existence and Christian existence, be indissolubly united.
He therefore sought to introduce Christianity into Christendom by
making it possible once more for Christendom to gain a decisive impression of this Christianity. At the same time, he also had to labor on behalf of man's proper humanity. Looking back on his work, he said that
he wanted to read once more for himself "the original text of the circumstances of individual, human existence, the old familiar tradition of
our fathers, and if possible interpret it more profoundly."

We have now outlined in brief how Kierkegaard looked upon the
introduction of Christianity into Christendom as his life's work and
have sketched the concomitant problems. But how did he set about this
task? Since Kierkegaard had studied theology and passed his theological
examinations, it was logical for him to become a clergyman or a professor of theology. But was it possible for him to hold ecclesiastical office
and at the same time ask the question with which he had to confront
Christendom, a question that was also the question of his own personal
life: do we who live within this secularized Christendom still have the
right to call ourselves Christians in the New Testament sense? This
question also implicated the church, asking whether instead of serving
the proclamation of the gospel the church was not withholding this very
gospel from mankind by refusing to take the illusion of "Christian"
history, of "Christian" civilization, of "Christian" society, of "Christian"
Christendom, and destroy it, as was the church's duty, preferring instead to live by this illusion. Kierkegaard therefore refused to take ecclesiastical office, and remained a self-employed writer. But this choice
only aggravated the problem of how he could communicate his insights
properly. He was dealing with a society that knew, not too little, but
rather too much, a society that, in this plethora of knowledge, had for-

gotten how to *exist*. It was therefore useless for him to communicate his own insights to this society as new knowledge. He was in the same situation as Socrates, who had first to destroy a false knowledge by means of his dialectic in order to elicit proper knowledge. For Kierkegaard, this proper knowledge is not knowledge *about* proper existence: it is proper existence itself. This fact transformed the question of the proper way to proceed into an extremely difficult problem of methodology for him. In order to solve it, he had to employ all the acumen of his dialectical passion. Like Socrates, he must transform human beings into individuals and communicate the existence based on faith to them in such a way that the recipient does not come to possess an item of knowledge through the communication, but is rather induced to achieve his own existence. To put it more precisely: the recipient must be able to accept the communication only in the stance of one who himself exists. Kierkegaard found the prototype for this method in Socrates, who, in his dialogues, can and must function only as a "midwife": he will help men to be delivered of the truth within them, but he cannot produce the truth for them by himself.

In this process, it is not only the recipient of the communication who matters, but always the communicator as well. Because the communicator seeks to help someone to achieve proper existence, proper existence is always demanded of him, also. What he does for another always affects his own training and development. And so Kierkegaard strove to find a way by which he could "train himself in truth and protect his life from the most terrible of all falsehoods, from having a disciple."

The Dialectic of Communication

We have heard what Kierkegaard said of Socrates, his model: Socrates was the first and only man "to give dialectical validity to the category of the individual." What does "dialectic" mean here? The original and simplest form of dialectic is conversation, dialogue. There must be at least two participants, neither of whom can arrive at the truth by himself. They seek instead to determine the truth by exchanging questions and answers, keeping their attention fixed on a common goal that determines the unity of question and answer. This form of dialectical conversation was Socrates' method, as illustrated by Plato in his first Dialogues. Socrates starts from the assumption that he himself does not know anything he can teach to anyone else, while his partner in the conversation obviously claims to know something. Now this supposed knowledge is tested in dialectic conversation; Socrates presses the attack until it becomes clear that the other man also does not know anything. The conversation ends with the apparently negative result that both admit, "I know that I do not know anything." But this negative result, in which false knowledge is destroyed, conceals a positive gain: the partner in the conversation has now been set free to know himself and to seek the fullness of truth within himself.

Kierkegaard took the original dialogic method of Socrates as his point of departure. In his Master's dissertation, *The Concept of Irony, with Special Reference to Socrates,* he worked out the form of this Socratic dialectic in contrast to that used later by Plato, who preserved only the external form of the dialogue without permitting any genuine questioning and answering. The dialectic of dialogue implies an attitude of irony in the questioner, behind which he conceals his own positivity in order to prevent any direct relationship from forming between the two men. In this fashion, the other man is set free to work out his own answers and the ideality of his existence is awakened. Irony is the incognito behind which takes place the total transformation demanded by this ideality. It is a "rule of existence; nothing is therefore more absurd than for a writer to express pleasure in having expressed himself ironically now and then. The man who really possesses irony possesses it as long as the day lasts, bound to a form, because it is infinity within him."

Now, like the Athenian Socrates, Kierkegaard also spent a great deal of his time in Socratic conversation upon the streets and among the societies of Copenhagen. The Danish Socrates, however, did what his Athenian counterpart did not do: he wrote books, an amazing quantity of books. One thing is always true of a book: it is a direct, didactic form of communication which has no control over the attitude of the reader. Kierkegaard, however, succeeded in remaining a Socratic ironist even when writing books. He did so by using a tremendous display of dialectic to transform the entire body of his writings into a single great dialogue with the reader. This explains the remarkable literary form he employed, which created a sensation even in 1843, when he published his first great work: *Either/Or: a Biographical Fragment, edited by Viktor Eremita.* The two volumes contain the posthumous papers of two different authors, which the editor claims to have found by accident in the secret compartment of a desk he had bought from an antique dealer. Since he could not determine the names of the authors, he refers simply to "the papers of A." and "the papers of B." The editor says of A.'s papers that they "contained diverse attempts to formulate an aesthetic philosophy of life," adding at once, "Such an attempt can probably not be brought off." Be that as it may, an effort is made with passionate consistency to carry these attempts through to the end. The papers of A. comprise all sorts of aphorisms, lyrical outpourings and reflections, discussions of eroticism, the erotic element in music, tragedy, etc., as well as lectures delivered before the *Symparanekromenoi* Society. The papers conclude with the "Diary of the Seducer," which A. claims not to have written himself, but only in turn to have edited, since the refinement of aesthetic pleasure displayed there has clearly become sinister in its own right. As an epigraph, the editor gives to the "papers of A." a quotation from Young: "Is reason alone baptized? Are the passions pagan?" The "papers of B." comprise letters written to A. by a certain Wilhelm, an assistant judge. They deal with "the aesthetic validity of marriage" and "the balance between the aesthetic and ethical elements in the development of the personality." In these letters, disagreeing with his friend A., he supports the claims of an ethical philosophy of life, closing with an "ultimatum," from which the entire work received its title *Either/Or*. He appends the sermon of another friend, on the subject, "The Edifying Value of the Thought That We Are Always in the Wrong Before God."

All these mystifications in literary form and in piling up of authors and editors of the documents serve the dialectic of communication. Kierkegaard does not appear before the reader as a teacher, trying to convince him of some philosophy through lecture and demonstration.

Instead, he publishes his books under pseudonyms, behind which his own person disappears. Each of these ever-changing pseudonyms represents a specific philosophy and attitude. They possess an inner consistency, representing a certain progress from an existence based on purely aesthetic principles through that based on ethics and religious ethics, culminating in the specifically Christian existence of the man of faith. The reader cannot directly appropriate the philosophy of the individual pseudonyms for the simple reason that the attitude of one figure is always contradicted ironically by that of the others. The reader can never reach a final conclusion backed by the authority of Kierkegaard himself. Kierkegaard disclaims all responsibility for the statements of his pseudonyms, demanding expressly that such statements should be quoted as coming from the pseudonym and not from himself. Kierkegaard says that he prefers to view himself "as the *reader,* rather than the *author*" of the documents, in order to prevent any possible misunderstanding that would place him in the role of a lecturer. In order to prevent this misunderstanding, for example, he has his psuedonymous Johannes Climacus say in the Foreword to the *Philosophical Fragments:*

> If anyone should be so polite as to attribute a point of view to me, if he should even stretch his gallantry to the limit and accept this point of view because it is mine, I regret his politeness, for he shows it to one who is unworthy. I also regret his point of view, if indeed he has no other point of view than mine. *My* life I can risk, *my* life in all seriousness I can wager, but not that of another. So much I am able to do;

it is all, indeed, that I can do, since I have no erudition to offer ... My life is all I have; I will risk it the instant a difficulty appears. Then the dance is easy; for the thought of death is a nimble dancer, my dancer; every human being is too heavy-footed for me; therefore I beseech you, *per deos obsecro,* not to ask me, for I will not dance.

In such statements, the reader must not see irony in the diction alone; he must understand it as the attitude behind which the speaker, like Socrates, conceals himself in order to set the person addressed free to achieve his own existence. The ironic form of expression can conceal everything; it restricts neither speaker nor listener to what is actually said. It can bring the listener to reveal himself; it can tempt him along a false trail in order to make him stumble at the end of this road and thus achieve insight. In any case, however, it must never allow the positivity it conceals to become visible. All this assumes, of course, that such a positivity is present. Irony is justified only when it conceals a strong passion for existence. Otherwise it ceases to be an attitude and becomes a rhetorical device, drifting off into petulance and thoughtlessness. Kierkegaard himself gives advice on how to avoid this danger:

If one wishes to undergo a healthy discipline, one should refrain for a while from the laughter that arouses the passion of antipathy where dark powers can so easily overpower one, and exercise instead the faculty of seeing the comic side of the person or thing toward which one feels protective, where sympathy and interest, or even partiality, constitute the active defense against recklessness.

Above all, be it noted, irony automatically ceases to be genuine when it is practiced not by an individual, but by the group. Kierkegaard's battle with the *Corsair* was directed against false, unjustified irony; with the assistance of this satirical paper, Copenhagen had become ironic *en masse,* and irony had been degraded into vulgarity.

Irony presupposes a very specific kind of intellectual training such as is very rare in this generation; and this chaos of human beings claim to be ironists! Irony is by definition nonsocial; an irony among the majority is by definition not irony.

Kierkegaard therefore had to declare war by himself against this false irony. He had to expose himself as an individual to this vulgarity in order to unmask it. Furthermore, he could not wage this war directly, but only ironically: he could not appear on the scene full of moral indignation, but had to issue a challenge to personal combat. The ironist must never directly reveal the value within him in order thus to win a person to the side of a truth. He must instead use all his talent to prevent any direct relationship with himself in order to bring his hearer to achieve his own existence, even if in the process he exposes himself to the accusation of thoughtlessness, of lack of seriousness, etc.

Kierkegaard's own conduct in this battle with the *Corsair* is a good example of this irony as an attitude. At the height of the dispute, when the paper had employed every means to make him ridiculous, Kierkegaard met Goldschmidt, the paper's editor, on the street. Kierkegaard did not engage in remonstrances, but spoke with him, as though not in the least personally involved, about the theoretical rights of Frater Taciturnus, the pseudonym under which Kierkegaard had issued his challenge. A short time later, Goldschmidt surrendered the editorship of the paper.

In Socratic dialectic, this ironic distance must be preserved not only for the sake of the person addressed, so that he is not persuaded of something but rather challenged to think and act for himself, but also for the sake of the speaker himself. This dialogue Kierkegaard conducts with the reader, using pseudonyms as a dodge, is also a dialogue with himself. His work as a writer also advances his own development. With extraordinary ability, both dialectic and poetic, he has the pseudonyms pace off the boundaries of humanity in order to retrieve faith from the realm of speculative philosophy and aesthetic sensitivity and restore it to real existence. Afterward, Kierkegaard saw in all the works he wrote a consistent plan that had not existed at the outset. Instead, "providence," as he put it, had itself educated him in its march of progress by means of this work. What he writes behind the mask of the pseudonyms are the possibilities of his own life, written in his own lifeblood. It is first of all himself whom he recalls to existence through this work.

Now of course all Copenhagen knew who the author of the pseudonymous works was. It was therefore unavoidable that the readers should lose the distance set between them and Kierkegaard by the pseudonyms, taking an interest in Kierkegaard as a person rather than limiting themselves to the pseudonyms. But this interest could cancel out all the irony of the Socratic dialectic and make it ineffectual. In order to prevent such a development, Kierkegaard snatched at yet another means to increase the indirectness of his communication: if he could not hide his person from the readers behind his work, he would have to disguise his person as much as possible. This meant that he had to take the same ironic attitude in his personal relationship to his environment that he took as a writer toward his readers.

His contemporaries in Copenhagen who had to come to terms with his work were therefore not given much personal information about him. Søren Kierkegaard was born on the 5th of May, 1813, the seventh and last child of Michael Pederson Kierkegaard, a wool merchant. In 1830, having been graduated with distinction from the local school, he matriculated at the University in Copenhagen. His way of life gave his contemporaries more the impression of an idler than of a serious young man. Only in 1840, after ten years of study, did he pass the theological examination, once more with distinction. In 1841, he received the degree of Master of Arts, having written a dissertation entitled *The Concept of Irony, with Special Reference to Socrates*. In the meantime, on the 10th of September, 1840, he had become engaged to Regine Olsen, the seventeen-year-old daughter of a prominent Copenhagen family. A year later he broke off the engagement without any reason discernible to society or even to his bride herself. He immediately traveled to Berlin to continue his studies. Upon his return, he began publishing his pseudonymous works. To the outside world his person was as great an enigma as the pseudonymous apparatus of his writing.

Today we know a bit more about him than his contemporaries did, primarily because we possess his very copious journals. We shall mention here only a few points that are important for the understanding of his work. While he was living the life of a well-situated private scholar, no one knew that he was publishing his books at his own expense and could calculate in advance the day on which his resources, which he had not invested, would be used up. Those contemporaries who knew him to be the author of the pseudonymous works could only assume that he wrote his books out of sheer pleasure in his own ability. They could have no inkling of the immense seriousness and tension of his life. When he challenged the *Corsair* in an apparent display of bravado, and it reacted as expected, no one noticed how deeply he suffered, not so much from the ridicule itself as from the despicable conduct of society, which immediately turned its back on him. The way he broke off his engagement without any apparent reason or concern scandalized the respectable citizens of Copenhagen. No one, not even his bride, could be allowed to suspect that he had been wrestling with God over the knowledge of his duty, and this struggle had taken him through hell and brought him to the very edge of insanity.

This account of his life will probably suggest that Kierkegaard was not a normal person. That is certainly true. He himself knew this better than anyone else. His own reactions made him suffer deeply: where his contemporaries could see no problem at all, his melancholy scrupulosity entangled him in the most complicated reflections, which he could never bring to issue in action. *Stages on Life's Way* contains a tale of woe called "Guilty? Not Guilty?" In it, Kierkegaard is describing himself when he has his pseudonym Quidam say:

> I see clearly that as a human being I am as far removed as possible from being paradigmatic. I am more a kind of human index. I indicate with some precision the temperature of every disposition and passion. In bringing forth my own inwardness, I understand the saying, *"Homo sum, nil humani a me alienum puto."* But in the human sense no one can imitate me. Still less am I prototypical in the historical sense for any man. I am rather such a person as might be found necessary in a crisis: a kind of human index, one who needs self-existence in order to grope his way forward.

A few biographical details should be added. All that we know about Kierkegaard himself suggests that his father's life, and one event in it particularly, was of extreme significance for him. Once when he was a poor shepherd boy twelve years old, on the moors of Jutland, Kierkegaard's father had cursed God on account of his wretched life. The memory of this event hounded the melancholy man, even when he later achieved respect and prosperity in Copenhagen; it drove him into a form of religious devotion in which only the sternest image of the crucified Lord could afford him comfort. In Søren, the "child of his old age," the father saw with clairvoyant dread his own history about to repeat itself. Then he did what he had to do: he brought his son, so perilously like him, under the same image of the crucified Lord; in the presence of this image he laid his own fate upon the shoulders of his son. When Kierkegaard is informed of this secret in the life of his father, suddenly, as he says, there is forced upon him "a new, infallible principle by which to interpret all phenomena": God's punishment lies upon the family as a curse. Even the most brilliant intellectual gifts must spell doom; only the Christian faith in its strictest form can open up new possibilities for a life weighed down by such a burden. From this moment on in Kierkegaard's life, the entire struggle of and for faith focused on this one point: it is, as he wrote in *The Sickness unto Death*, "if you like, a frantic struggle for possibility." How is it possible—so goes his question —for a man to emerge once more into freedom if the heavy burden of his past has already forestalled the free possibility of the future? We can also state the question simply in these terms: how is the forgiveness of sins made possible, and how can a man really live by grace? To Kierkegaard, it was no accident that the "forgiveness of sins" and the "resurrection of the body" are juxtaposed in the Creed. What is made *new* through faith in the forgiveness of sins is the *old* man, not someone else. A man does not become a blank page. What he realizes in his new life are possibilities lying in his own past history, even if he has already bungled them.

All this has nothing whatever to do with any pietistic conversion and subjectivity. It was not Kierkegaard's intent, even if he had been able, to take refuge from the old man in a life of subjective contemplation totally unrelated to the *vita ante acta*. Faith rather holds a person to his own past history, which is run backward and made transparent. The important thing is firmly to confront one's former life with repentance. Kierkegaard makes no distinction between individual and hereditary guilt, and demands that a man assume penitently the guilt of his forefathers. And this life history is now lived forward through faith in forgiveness; this faith realizes all the possibilities within a person, realizes them within the human sphere in all its breadth and depth. "Spatial and temporal limitation—that is what everything hinges on," Kierkegaard had his Johannes de silentio say. This limitation cannot be denied through an abstract life of "sanctification," in which a man escapes from his own past history. Through such a life, a man becomes not himself but a caricature of himself, a caricature reduced to certain specific religious possibilities. The life of faith is rather that existence which, with controlled passion, realizes its own possibility by living by grace. This existence was the goal of all Kierkegaard's work. His primary task was to train himself for this existence; and, through his work, he sought to make it as accessible to others as was humanly possible.

This discussion shows clearly why, in Kierkegaard's case, the thinker's person and his work are indissolubly linked in a way that holds true for scarcely any other man. At the same time, it has also made clear how in his case the work has so absorbed the person that the person can vanish completely behind it. In this "frantic struggle of faith for possibility," Kierkegaard worked out universally applicable categories by which to govern his own singular life. In this way he exhibited the rule in himself, the exception. He has Quidam say:

> With all the strength at my command I force myself to hold my life to its proper category. A man can die, I know; a man can die a martyr's death, I know; but a man can hold to his category, can adhere to his category. This is what I myself seek, what I demand of everyone that I admire, of everyone that I even recognize: by day he must think on the category of his life, and dream of it by night.

By "category," Kierkegaard means the objectively valid norms under which being appears to thought. For him, the "being" in question is the reality of his own existence; the categories are therefore to him the universally valid basic concepts of thought, through which the individual who has achieved existence consciously governs his life.

What Kierkegaard writes is self-confession through and through, but it is confession objectified to such a degree that the prayer "I will not let thee go, except thou bless me" is audible only to the man whom Kierkegaard's work blinds to the author's person and compels to achieve his own existence. At one point in his *Journal,* Kierkegaard writes:

> If the tribunal of knowledge is to come into play, a man must venture forth into life, must out to sea and let his cry resound, whether God will hear it or no. He must not stand upon the shore and watch the others struggle and contend. Only thus does knowledge come before the bar. There is truly a world of difference between standing on one's legs and proving God's existence, and thanking him on one's knees.

And so, despite the complete irregularity of Kierkegaard's life, his work can not only interest, it must also challenge us to take a position with regard to it. It is not the man himself that puts us under this obligation, but the category to which he adheres. "Every existence that seeks after something," continues Quidam in the passage cited, "indirectly becomes a judgment upon the others; and whoever seeks after the category judges indirectly him who does not seek after it." Only the man who meets this aggressive challenge issued to the reader by Kierkegaard's work can, perhaps, afterward inquire about Kierkegaard's own life under these categories. Then, of course, he will no longer be interested in whether it was a "normal" human being who established them, but only in whether they are right. Their rightness will be confirmed by the fact that they are able to comprehend even such a burdened life as that of Kierkegaard.

But did they help Kierkegaard himself to achieve that freedom in which a man can realize what is universally human? He himself sought the answer to this question throughout his life, especially with regard to the rightness of canceling his engagement when he thought that his "thorn in the flesh" would not let him follow this universal path. A few years later, he wrote in his *Journal:* "Had I had faith, I would have stayed with Regine. Thanks be to God, I can see that now. During those days I came close to losing my senses." Or again: "My sin is that I did not have faith, faith in the fact that for God, all things are possible—but," he then continued, "where is the dividing line between this and tempting God?" The answering of this question was unable to bring forth any additional category from Kierkegaard. Throughout his entire life he wrestled for an answer in this dismal battle for the boundary between faith and temptation. This battle, however, is not for the eyes of curious spectators. Whoever would share properly in this fight can once more only allow Kierkegaard to ask him how he himself, with the thorn in his own flesh, would properly deal with the battle between faith and temptation.

The Poet of Christianity

Kierkegaard saw the reintroduction of Christianity into Christendom as his life's work. He was of the opinion that it was impossible in the present secularized state of Christendom to gain any impression whatsoever of the passion of the Christian faith. A wealth of information about Christianity had caused men to forget what it means to *exist* as a Christian. At the same time, men had also lost the necessary passion for existing as *human beings*. Both therefore had to be restored at the same time; for a Christianity that does not live by the passion of faith is invariably also a deeply inhuman affair.

Socrates served as Kierkegaard's great model in the fulfillment of this task: Socrates, who used his dialogic method to free men from their false knowledge in order to release the truth within them. We have seen how Kierkegaard imitated this Socratic procedure through the literary form of his works, by using the apparatus of pseudonymity to transform all his work as a writer into one single great Socratic dialogue with the reader. We have also seen how he hid his own person ironically behind this work in order to prevent any direct communication between himself and the reader, thereby transmuting his singular personal life into universally valid categories.

Now this method of indirect communication with the aid of Socratic irony contained a difficulty for the "Danish Socrates" that did not exist for his Athenian precursor. The latter's procedure lived on the assumption that every man can and must find the truth within himself. The important thing was therefore merely to release this inner truth by encouraging every man to rely on his own efforts in his search for truth. Socrates therefore said that he could only "function as a midwife" for men, and that "bearing witness" is a task that falls to God himself.

Kierkegaard, however, sought to do more than refer each man to the truth he can find within himself because, as the Greek puts it, he has it in his "memory." His goal was rather to assist each man in achieving the Christian existence of faith. The object of this faith, however, is not a truth that a man has within himself, that he might find in his own memory; it concerns instead "what no eye has seen, nor ear heard, nor the heart of man conceived," what is true only because, contrary to all human expectation, God brought it to pass by revealing himself in Jesus Christ. The truth to which Socrates sought to lead men lies within the sphere of human immanence; to discover this truth, therefore, it suffices that it set the individual's own intellect in motion. The Christian truth, however, which Kierkegaard sought to inculcate cannot be attained in this manner because it lies beyond all human possibilities. Its truth, the revelation, is a historical event that must first be communicated directly to a man in order that he may draw the proper conclusions for his own existence.

This, then, was Kierkegaard's difficulty: he had to work this direct communication of the Christian relevation into his indirect Socratic form of communication. And he had to do this in such a way that the receiver of this communication, i.e., the reader of Kierkegaard's writings, might not only receive some information about the facts of Christianity (the reader already knew far too much about Christianity, or at least thought he knew it); the communication had to proceed in such a way that the reader would not only be *instructed* about Christianity, but would also be *urged to be* a Christian.

To start with, Kierkegaard tried to solve this problem by letting his pseudonyms introduce the existential possibility of the Christian faith alongside various others. Just as he had the pseudonyms give literary reality to the aesthete and moral philosopher, just as they transformed his own fate into literature in order to illustrate the categories of existence for the reader, so also they gave literary reality to existence based on Christian faith. This had been his ultimate purpose all along, but he had not declared it openly at the start. Instead, as he put it on one occasion, he tried to "trick men into truth." Indirectly, however, he had already betrayed his intention in a remarkable fashion from the outset. Three months after *Either/Or,* the first of his pseudonymous works, appeared, he published under his own name *Two Edifying Discourses.*

These were followed during the next few years by many more, which were published to accompany the pseudonymous works; later, he called these "Christian" discourses. In these discourses Kierkegaard offered with his right hand what he had offered with his left in the pseudonymous works. Here he addressed the reader directly, without any ironic concealment. In evaluating Kierkegaard's work, most people have overlooked the significance of these discourses, concerning themselves only with the pseudonymous writings. Martin Heidegger is an outstanding exception on this point. Heidegger says that it is even possible to learn more in the philosophical sense from Kierkegaard's "edifying" writings than from his theoretical writings, with the exception of *The Concept of Dread*. We shall therefore return to a detailed examination of these discourses, in which Kierkegaard gave with his right hand. First, though, we must ask how he gave literary form to the Christian life in his pseudonymous works—in other words, where he gave with his left hand.

In October of 1843—half a year after the appearance of *Either/Or*—there appeared two works, *Fear and Trembling: Dialectical Poetry, by Johannes de silentio* and *Repetition: an Experiment in Experimental Psychology, by Constantin Constantius*. We may recall that the existential possibilities presented by Kierkegaard through the pseudonyms were primarily those of his own existence, aberrations from the norm whereby one might say that he went through the paradigm of general human existence. In these two writings he did so in a very special way. The problems they present seem at first rather remote; to understand these problems, we must view them against the background of *Either/Or*. In *Either/Or*, Kierkegaard contrasted aesthetic and ethical existence, bringing the two existential possibilities to a confrontation primarily in their different attitudes toward eroticism and toward marriage. The aesthete A. is concerned to experience anew in each fresh experience of love the immediacy of first love. What he fears most, therefore, is that his love might acquire continuity and thereby a history. We see this fear particularly clearly, for example, at the conclusion of the "Diary of the Seducer." After he has induced the girl to break off the engagement of her own accord, so that no restrictions may detract from the erotic relationship, and to surrender herself to him freely, he drops her and writes in his diary:

Why cannot such a night continue longer? If Alektryon could over-sleep, why cannot the sun? But now it is gone; I want never to see her again. When a girl has surrendered everything, she has lost everything. In a man, innocence is a negative concept; in a woman, it is the very essence of her nature. Now all resistance is past; and only while there is serious resistance to overcome is it beautiful to love. When resistance ends, love becomes weakness and wont. I do not want to be reminded of my relationship with her. She has lost her fragrance, and the time is past when a girl could transform herself into a heliotrope through grief over a faithless lover. I have no intention of saying farewell. I find a woman's tears and entreaties offensive: they alter everything but change nothing. I loved her, but from now on she is of no concern to my soul. If I were a god, I would do for her what Neptune did for a nymph: I would transform her into a man.

What he puts into the mouth of B., the moral philosopher, sounds ingenuous and prosaic. In his letters to A. about "The Aesthetic Validity of Marriage," B. writes:

Married love is thus both commonplace and divine; and it is divine because it is commonplace. Married love does not come with outward signs. It does not parade its presence with sound and fury; it is the steadfast nature of a quiet spirit. Of this latter, you, like all conquering natures, can have no idea. Your kind are always immersed in themselves and always beside themselves. As long as every nerve within you vibrates, while, as you put it, you are on the prowl for booty, and the janissary music within you deafens your conscience, then it seems to you that you are living. But when the battle is won, when the final echo of the final shot has died away, when your quick thoughts like orderlies hasten back to headquarters and report that victory is yours, then you do not know how to begin; for now you are facing the real beginning for the first time. What you call "wont" and abhor as an unavoidable consequence of marriage is merely the historical aspect of marriage, which, to your perverted eye, takes on such a dangerous appearance.

The aesthete supposes that the habitual wont arising out of marriage profanes love. He says:

How disgusting it is to observe the languor with which all this takes place in married life, how superficially, how indolently it happens, almost according to the clock, rather like the tribe the Jesuits found in

Paraguay, which was so indolent that the Jesuits considered it necessary to have a bell rung at midnight to give all husbands a pleasant reminder of their conjugal duties. Everything takes place *a tempo,* as in a trained animal.

In the face of this caricature, the moral philosopher stresses the significance of *time,* which gives history and continuity to married love. Recollection and hope merge, so that the high point does not lie *behind* the lovers as a past event, the way it does for the aesthetic representative of "first love," but instead always lies *before* them as a possibility, perpetually renewed. In marriage, true love lives on the possibility of repetition—in other words, on just what the aesthete fears so terribly. The moral philosopher, on the contrary, can say that he, too, preserves the aesthetic element, because the important thing is not to *represent* what is aesthetically beautiful, but to *live* an aesthetically beautiful life. In this sense it is not romantic love but married love that must be called aesthetically beautiful.

B., the moral philosopher of *Either/Or,* extends this confrontation between aesthetics and ethics beyond the specific question of the relationship between love and marriage. In his letters on "The Equilibrium Between Aesthetics and Ethics in the Development of the Personality," he gives it universal application. Here, too, the important thing is not to destroy the aesthetic element, but rather to absorb it in the ethical element in such a way that it is preserved. The controversy between the two culminates here in the problem of *obligation.* The aesthete resists obligation because he looks upon it as something imposed upon him from without to compel him to do something; the moral philosopher, on the contrary, tries to show him that a man's obligations lie within him. He uses the phenomenon of conscience as an illustration, saying:

> This is the mystery that lies within the conscience, this mystery that shrouds the life of the individual: it is at once particular and universal— if not immediately per se, then at least potentially.

Now obligation consists in the expression of what is universally human by each particular individual in his own life. No one, though, can express what is universally human by divesting himself of his fortuitous concrete individuality; this would mean becoming nothing at all. One must instead consciously assume responsibility for one's own concrete individuality and permeate it with what is universal.

> When, therefore, the ethical individual has completed his task, when he has fought the good fight, then he has arrived at the point of having become an individual. This means there is no other person like him and he has also become universal man.

This passage obviously presupposes that every man has within him the possibility of becoming universal man. What he already *is* potentially he must also now *become* by his own free decision, by choosing himself in his own concrete individuality as his ethical goal. Thus he lives in continuity with himself and with his environment by developing within himself the personal and the civic virtues. Now the universal goal which it is one's obligation to realize is not fixed; it is subject to all kinds of historical change. On this point, the moral philosopher says:

> It is significant that our very idiom takes this skepticism into account. I never say of a man that he carries out obligation or obligations; I say instead that he carries out *his* obligations, I carry out *my* obligations, you carry out *your* obligations . . . I do not at all see that this means the world must founder in skepticism; for the difference between good and evil remains forever constant, as do responsibility and obligation, even if no man can tell me what *my* obligation is. Everyone can always know what *his own* obligation is, however. This would not be the case if the unity of the universal and the individual were not established.

Our task, therefore, is never to set up as a universal obligation something outwardly ascertainable, definite, a casuistry of individual obligations. We are dealing instead with something internal, with the intensity of the sense of obligation with which the individual takes responsibility for himself as universal man.

> When the personality has experienced with its entire energy the intensity of obligation, it is ethically mature; obligation will then arise within the personality itself. The important thing is therefore not that a man be able to count up his obligations on his fingers, but that he have experienced once and for all the intensity of obligation, that consciousness of this intensity have become to him a foreknowledge of the eternal validity of its nature . . . Let casuistry busy itself with working out the multitude of obligations; the important thing, the one thing

necessary, is and shall remain that, in respect to his own life, a man be not its uncle, but its father.

For comparison, let us cite another passage from *Stages on Life's Way*, 1845, "Various Thoughts on Marriage Against Objections, by a Married Man." Here the case is considered of someone who escapes this "Either/Or" by evasion, becoming neither a seducer nor a married man. As an example of such a "hybrid existence" the author cites Goethe, as Goethe described himself in *Dichtung und Wahrheit*. Here, he says,

an existence is depicted that is not the existence of a seducer; it is too gallant for that, even if this gallantry is inferior to that of a seducer when judged according to its spirit (understood ethically), because the crucial decision is missing; for even a demonic decision is ethical, *viz.*, ethically evil. Such an existence is more easily pardoned by the world, in fact all too easily, for the person in question is really in love. But then—then his ardor cools, he was mistaken, he takes his leave "with happy mien." Half a year later he can give reasons, good reasons, why the breakup and his absence were sensible and almost commendable: it was really nothing, she was only a pretty little country girl, too much passion was involved and passion does not endure in the long run, and so on . . . With the help of half a year and with the help of perspective, the fact of love has become a mere happenstance, escape from which makes the man a hero . . . That we are dealing here with run-of-the-mill love stories is hardly the fault of the female participants. All honor to Goethe's description, whether it be poetry or truth; for, so far as I can remember, there is no reason to suppose that a single one of these stories became vaudeville instead of tragedy. If a pretty little country girl had the misfortune to mistake His Excellency while remaining true to herself, I learned in school and have never learned better, she is promoted: what was an idyll becomes a tragedy. If, however, His Excellency had the misfortune to mistake himself, and, what is worse, to behave in such a way as to try to make amends, I learned in school and have never learned better, we have left the realm of tragedy and drama and settled in vaudeville.

The question of the author, which is also Kierkegaard's question, is directed at finding out the sense in which the poetic figure from *Dichtung und Wahrheit* can serve as a paradigm for what is universally human. He says:

Such an existence is not a paradigm in the strict sense; but it can still

take on paradigmatic character in the figurative sense or even be for-
tuitously paradigmatic, so that it is an irregular declension, which the
lives of most men follow. These people cannot be said to shape their
lives according to this paradigm; for that they are too innocent. This is
precisely their excuse: they find themselves in these circumstances and
do not know themselves how it happens. Often such men are even fa-
natics pursuing an ideal. No more than the man who buys a lottery
ticket learns from losing do these men learn from having loved.

Here the paradigm takes a dangerous turn, leading to that enormously
popular hybrid existence which avoids the "Either/Or." One might ask,
however, whether Goethe does not constitute an exception on this point,
precisely because he is a poet. In fact, the question of the justifiable
exception to the universal rule is what concerned Kierkegaard continually.

In reply, the author says:

I did not presume to decide the extent to which every poet's existence
should be itself a poem, nor to determine the proper angle of refrac-
tion between a poet's life and his poetry. This much is certain: an
existence such as *Dichtung und Wahrheit* depicts must have some influence on what a poet produces. If it is Goethe who is here recounting
his own life, we have an apparent explanation for the fact that what
Goethe seems most to lack is fervor. He does not have the fervor of immediacy; he is too prudent. Neither did he succeed in achieving the
highest fervor. Each time a crisis arrives he dodges it. He dodges in
every possible direction.

Here the author singles out the way Goethe disposes of religious questions: he emphasizes the deep religious impressions of his youth, but
makes no use of them in overcoming these crises later in his life. This
leads the author to say:

If this poet is Goethe himself, does this then not explain the fact that
the idolized hero whose chance utterances are collected, published, discussed, and read like sacred relics, this idolized hero who is called king
of the intellectual world, is, to put it mildly, a mere titular king in the
eternal realm of religiosity?

Now this poet considered himself a "privileged individual," and had
no desire to be an instructive example for others. For the sake of his
existence as a poet, he could afford, he *had* to afford, to behave in such

a peculiar fashion and devise the circumstances of his life as though it were a poem. But this argument does not impress our author, and he replies:

> How many dabblers and hacks have crept past this peculiarity of nature, bowing in admiration? And yet every man possesses this peculiarity of nature to some degree. It is quite simple: the natural, greedy man's way of parrying the thrusts of ethics.

He therefore goes on to say:

> If this poet's existence in *Dichtung und Wahreit* is poetic, then there is no place for marriage; it is at best a refuge for one's declining years. If that existence is poetic, what is to be done with the woman? It is ugly enough when a man tried and tested in erotic adventure, experienced, and now ready to retire, takes a young girl as his wife to rejuvenate him a little and give him the best of care now that he is beginning to grow old. But it is disgusting when a mature woman, an experienced virgin, marries a young man to provide herself a refuge and the stimulus of expertise—then the poetry begins to evaporate . . . What Solomon says strikes me as being more poetic: whoever finds a wife receives a wonderful gift from God; or, to modernize the idiom a little, God looks with favor on the man who has fallen in love. If he marries the woman he loves, he performs a good work and brings to a proper conclusion what he has begun.

The author adds:

> This latter point is naturally not intended as a wretched excuse for the decision to marry. Marriage is its own best recommendation; for, as has been said, it is the only adequate form that love can take.

The author also gives serious thought to whether there can be any justifiable exception, whether a man may properly consider himself dispensed from the realization of the universal. The guiding principle is: "He must not feel himself to be superior to the universal. He must desire to continue in the universal *à tout prix*." Life itself must force a man into an exceptional existence against his will, and he must suffer for it. "The exception cannot purchase its justification for a round sum; it must pay the price to the last penny." And most important of all: at the moment of his decision, the man who decides for an exceptional existence must not know whether he is really the justified exception.

Such an exception to what is universally human as Goethe's "hybrid existence" halfway between the aesthetic and the ethical is, in any case, quite out of the question. But the question of a justifiable exception to the universal demands of ethics continues to plague Kierkegaard. The reason is obvious: he himself did not marry Regine Olsen, thus disregarding the words he put in the mouth of the author: "If he marries the woman he loves, he performs a good work and brings to a proper conclusion what he has begun." Nor is this the only point at which Kierkegaard's life fails to follow the map he had the moral philosopher lay out in *Either/Or*. The exhortation to lead an ethical life such as we found represented by that philosopher continues in force: in every instance Kierkegaard is concerned to realize the universal in his individual life. But we must also take into account the obstacles standing in the way of any realization of the ethical demand which transform the "good fight" of the moral philosopher, which strives to realize what is universally human, into that "frantic struggle for possibility." These obstacles differ for each man to the extent that the individuality of each man, which obstructs his realization of the universal, is not the result of natural processes and therefore a neutral condition; each man must bear responsibility for what he has grown to be.

Here we encounter the vast problem of guilt and fate. If a man seeks to come to terms with what he has grown to be, he must first of all deal with a fate that has placed him outside the circle of what is universally human. He must ask what role God plays in this fate, he must ask whether and to what extent God himself dispensed him by this fate from realizing what is universally human.

God and Fate

We encounter the question of God's role in fate in connection with the question of whether and to what extent a man can be dispensed from realizing the ethical demand of what is universally human. This question is examined in the two works *Fear and Trembling* and *Repetition*.

Fear and Trembling: Dialectical Poetry, by Johannes de silentio seeks, using Abraham as an example, to show what *faith* is.

> Through faith Abraham forsook his fatherland and became an alien in the land of promise. One thing he left behind, and one thing he took along. He left behind his worldly wits, and took faith along. Otherwise he probably would never have emigrated, but would have thought: But this is madness! ... Through faith Abraham received the promise that in his seed all nations of the earth should be blessed ... And Abraham became old, Sarah became the laughingstock of the region; and yet he was God's elect and heir of the promise that in his name all nations should be blessed. Abraham believed in the promise, and that means he believed in it for *this* life. If his faith had only been directed toward a future life, it would have been easier for him to discard everything in order to hasten from this world to which he did not belong. But such a faith was not the faith of Abraham—if, indeed, such a faith exists ... Abraham's faith was in this very life; he had faith that his life would be long in the land, honored among the people, blessed in his nation, remembered in Isaac, whom he embraced as his dearest treasure ...

Abraham had kept this faith in his struggle with that cunning and vigilant enemy who never slumbers, in his struggle with time, "with that ancient figure who survives us all," and he had received Isaac. But now,

all the terrors of the contest were concentrated in a single moment: And
God did tempt Abraham, and said unto him: Take your son, your only
son Isaac, whom you love, and go to the land of Moriah, and offer him
there as a burnt offering upon one of the mountains of which I shall tell
you.

Even now, Abraham had faith and did not doubt: "he had faith in what
reason denied." He still had faith in the promise for *this* life.

There he stood, the old man, with his only hope. But he did not doubt;
he did not look nervously to right and left; he did not challenge heaven
with his prayers. He knew that the one who was testing him was the al-
mighty God; he knew that it was the costliest sacrifice that could be
demanded of him; but he knew also that no sacrifice is too costly if
God demands it, and—he drew the knife.

Thus, as Johannes de silentio says, Abraham in his faith is "great
through the power whose strength is weakness; great through the wisdom whose secret is foolishness; great through the hope whose form is
madness; great through the love that is hatred toward itself." And all
this took place in order that "souls in dread might have a star to guide
them to deliverance."

And wherein does the *dread** of those souls consist, those souls of
whom Kierkegaard was himself an outstanding example?

Abraham's action, ethically speaking, is this: he sought to *murder*
Isaac; religiously speaking, he sought to *sacrifice* Isaac. But just this contradiction is the source of that dread which can easily rob a man of his sleep;
and yet Abraham would not be who he is without this dread.

But this story would not be worth discussing were it only the account
of an event in the past, which can never enter into the present. This entry
into the present takes place when, moved by faith, a man gives up what
is finite, not to lose it, but rather, by virtue of absurdity, to gain it for
the first time fully and completely. For "everything hinges on limitations
of time and space."

The author's purpose, as he puts it, is

to draw out the dialectical element contained in the story of Abraham
and develop it in the form of problems in order to show what a mon-

---

* Translator's note: "dread" is used here and elsewhere not in its usual English sense,
but simply as a conventional translation of the German *Angst.*

strous paradox faith is: a paradox that can turn a murder into a holy act, pleasing to God; a paradox that returns Isaac to Abraham; a paradox that no thinking can master, because faith begins just where thinking leaves off.

The first question is, "Can there be a teleological suspension of ethical demands?" That is, can a higher *telos* or purpose suspend the universal demands of ethics upon a man, as in the case of Abraham? Such suspension is impossible within the limits of ethical idealism, where the universal demands of ethics are themselves the divine element. Abraham, on the contrary, has "a private relationship to the deity," which cannot exist within the limits of philosophical ethics, or, for that matter, within the limits of paganism. In such a world Abraham could be understood only as a tragic hero. Here would lie his undeniable greatness, and the observer could mourn his tragic fate. But, says the author, "it is impossible to mourn for Abraham. One approaches him with a *horror religiosus* like that of Israel approaching Mount Sinai." Here, as a result of his private relationship to God, a man as an individual stands higher than the universal. A question confronts the observer: does Abraham deserve respect and esteem as a "cavalier of faith," or must he be banished into exile as a presumptive murderer? This question confronts not only the observer, but also Abraham himself. How can he be certain that, in his ghastly decision to sacrifice Isaac, he is not sinning, but is justified as the singular exception? He cannot appeal to the denouement, which will vindicate him, for he must obey the command without knowing the denouement. Neither can he turn to flesh and blood for counsel, for he cannot speak a word about his charge. He can only rely on the passion of faith, which bears its proof within itself; for, says the author,

> he who treads the narrow way of faith has no one who might give him counsel, no one who might understand him. Faith is a miracle, and yet no man is barred from it; for passion is common to all, and faith is a passion.

The second question that the author poses is, "Can there be an absolute obligation toward God?" Consider the case of Abraham: his relationship to the universal does not determine his relationship to the absolute; as a singular individual he has an absolute relationship to the absolute.

This is what it means to say that he has a private relationship to the deity. Abraham's concern can no longer be subsumed under the heading of what moral philosophers, somewhat innocuously, are wont to call "conflict of obligations." What is demanded of him lies beyond any possible ethical obligation. Ethics can only condemn him as a murderer. Within the realm of ethics, there can be no possibility of deliverance for him. He can be delivered only if, as the author puts it, "love of God can compel the cavalier of faith to express his love of his neighbor in a way completely contrary, ethically speaking, to what obligation demands." One could also state it thus: if the ethical demand of the universal is supreme, and not faith, then Abraham is lost.

Now of course it can always be a temptation that is seeking to persuade the individual to transgress the limits of the universal; in this case, he should withstand this temptation. But only the individual can decide whether he is being tempted or whether, through his faith, he is the justified exception and must therefore act accordingly. No one can relieve him of the burden of this decision, but neither can he justify himself and his decision in anyone's eyes. It is possible, however, to distinguish the true cavalier of faith from the counterfeit: the counterfeit joins a sect comprising like-minded individuals, while the true cavalier of faith is brought into absolute isolation. The author writes:

> That is the dreadful fate that the sectarian weakling cannot bear. Instead of learning from his isolation that *he* is *unable* to carry out his great plans and admitting this fact freely (a course of which I can only approve, since I follow it myself), the incompetent fellow thinks he would be able to carry out his plans if he could join together with a few other incompetents. Now a dozen or so sectarians are strutting about arm in arm. They naturally have no inkling of the temptation that prevents the cavalier of faith from exercising his "faith" so companionably *con amore*. Whatever dread may rear its ugly head they drown out through a raucous boasting of their "faith." And this brawling mob thinks it can walk the same path as the cavalier of faith, who, alone in the solitude of the universe with his terrible responsibility, never hears a human voice. But in the world of the spirit there can be no cheating. Without the agony of temptation the bliss of faith cannot exist.

Thus Kierkegaard had his pseudonym Johannes de silentio illustrate what faith is by the example of Abraham. But why did he do this?

What was he trying to say? And to whom was he trying to say it? We may recall Kierkegaard's opinion that it was no longer possible, within a world turned "Christian," to gain any impression of the passion of the Christian faith. So he tried to communicate this impression to the reader while keeping his distance in pseudonymity by depicting Christianity as a poet. The crucial point is not that he chose the literary form of "dialectical poetry," as he did here in *Fear and Trembling*. We shall see that he could do the same thing in strictly scientific form, which is completely different. He spoke as a "poet" because he was neither willing nor able to be himself a witness to his faith. Otherwise he would have had to speak differently. For, says Johannes de silentio,

> the true cavalier of faith is always a witness, never a teacher; therein lies the profound feeling for humanity that is rather more important than that loquacious sharing of other people's joy and sorrow which is usually so highly esteemed as sympathy, but is actually nothing more than *vanity*. Whoever seeks to be a witness confesses thereby that no man, not even the most humble, needs the sympathy of another which only degrades the one in order that the other may rise. But since he himself did not gain what is his cheaply, neither will he sell it cheaply.

Here, too, the question arises to which we shall continue to devote serious attention, the crucial problem of Kierkegaard's life: is it really possible for a man to speak of Christianity merely as a poet without having to become a personal witness to his faith? In his pseudonymous works, Kierkegaard at first thought this was a possible option. But anyone who can read with the slightest sensitivity, if he studies this "dialectical poetry" in which the tone in which something is said is so enormously important, will hear at once through it the passion of a speaker who is himself wavering in dread between faith and temptation; a speaker who, in the entire dialectical development of the problem of Abraham, sees and seeks nothing but the great example, by which, as we have heard, Abraham provides for "souls in dread . . . a star to guide them to deliverance." The distance provided by the pseudonyms is certainly not intended to prevent our hearing *this*. Indeed, its real purpose is rather to assist us, if we understand correctly why Kierkegaard prefers to view himself only as a reader and not as the author of his writings.

At the same time as *Fear and Trembling,* there appeared also *Repe-*

tition: an Experiment in Experimental Psychology, by Constantin Constantius. It is concerned once more with the problem of the justified exception and its relationship to the ethical universal. The author develops this problem through the love story of a young man whose love makes him a poet, thereby making him unsuitable for married life. The woman he loves has become for him the poet's muse. For him, this leads to a magnificent expansion of his possibilities; for her, however, it becomes an affront to the element of *eros.* It is the same problem we have seen illustrated by the example of Goethe in *Stages on Life's Way.* But Constantin Constantius can no longer dispose of the problem as simply as did the ethical supporter of marriage in the latter work, who could not admit an exception to the universal even in the case of the poet. The young man in Constantin Constantius' experiment cannot be dismissed so quickly as a "hybrid existence," like the Goethe of *Dichtung und Wahrheit,* who neither married nor became a seducer, but became an "expert" in erotic love. The young man whose love has made him a poet is granted the point that "a poet is, in general, an exception." Since he cannot marry without surrendering his poetic calling, the justified exception becomes a legitimate problem, because he suffers profoundly from this conflict with the universal. It is no longer possible to give him the simple answer that was given to the husband, that "God looks with favor on the man who has fallen in love. If he marries the woman he loves, he performs a good work and brings to a proper conclusion what he has begun."

Now this "good work" appears considerably more problematical; and the author has this to say about the significance of the exception:

> The universal itself embodies a strange conflict between the anger and impatience evoked by the uproar that the exception gives rise to and an affectionate partiality toward the exception. For in the end the universal rejoices over an exception just as heaven rejoices more over one sinner who repents than over ninety and nine who need no repentance.

Of course this does not hold true for the unjustified exception, which is distinguishable by its desire to evade the universal. The justified exception, however, is the best place to study the universal, because by explaining itself it also explains what is common to all.

The young man of the experiment does not succeed in making his peace with the universal; he remains trapped in the existence of a poet. When he finally decides to marry, the woman he loves has already married someone else. But the significance of the experiment lies in the way the border-conflicts that lead to faith are fought out. This time Job is the biblical prototype. For Job did not stop with saying, "The LORD gave, and the LORD has taken away; blessed be the name of the LORD." After he had remained silent for seven days and seven nights, the passionate tumult within him burst forth: he became "the mouth of the sufferer, the sigh of the oppressed, the cry of him who dreads"; he became "a relief to all who suffer silently, a faithful witness for all the misery that can dwell in the heart of man." He dared, "an incorruptible advocate for man, embittered in his soul, to lodge his complaint and dispute with God." "Why does everyone conceal this?" asks the young man; whereupon he says:

> Woe to him . . . who would cunningly deprive the grief-stricken of the temporary consolation of grief, the chance to gain a breathing space and "dispute with God." Or has the fear of God become so great in our days that the grief-stricken man no longer needs the custom of days gone by? . . . Therefore speak, immortal Job! Repeat all that you have said, you mighty advocate, standing intrepid as a roaring lion before the judgment seat of the Most High! In your words is strength, in your heart is fear of God, even when you complain, when you guard your despair against your friends, who rise up like thieves and fall upon you with their thoughts . . . It is you I require, a man who knows how to voice complaint so loud that it resounds through heaven, where God takes counsel with the devil, devising plots against a man. Present your case, the Lord is not afraid, he can defend himself quite well. But why should he defend himself when no one dares to lodge complaint, as befits a man? Speak, lift up your voice, speak loudly. Of course God can speak more loudly; after all, he has the thunder—but even thunder is an answer, an explanation, reliable, true, primordial, an answer from God himself. Though it destroy a man, it is more glorious than the gossip of the city, more glorious than any prattle about righteous governance, the invention of human wisdom, disseminated by old women and semi-men.

"Job's secret, his driving force, his nerve, his one idea, is this: despite everything, he is in the right." He therefore demands "to be considered an exception to the rule; his endurance and his strength prove his claim is warranted." He will admit no human explanation for his misfortune; he insists on a hearing with the Lord, declaring himself to be pure and innocent. Nor does he stifle his passion by allowing himself to believe that he must suffer on account of his sins; to do so would be to turn God into a tyrant.

> Job stands by his declaration that he is in the right. He does so in such a way as to bear witness to that noble human candor that knows what man is, knows that man, though fragile and delicate as a flower, is still made great by his freedom, knows that in this freedom man has a knowledge that cannot be snatched away, not even by the God who gave it to him. At the same time, Job maintains his conviction in such a way that one can see in him the loving confidence that is convinced that God could clear up all the difficulties if only he could be induced to speak.

But if Job is in the right, how are we to explain his fate? It is sometimes called a *test*. But this, too, involves great difficulties. Within what realm of knowledge should this "test" be categorized? It does not belong to aesthetics or to ethics or to dogmatic theology; it transcends all these definitions.

> It makes man oppose God on a purely personal level. It makes it impossible for a man to be content with a second-hand explanation. There are people who immediately produce the category of a "test" when the going gets rough; but this only proves that they do not understand anything about a test.

Job came to understand what it means to be tested only after frightful suffering. Unlike Abraham, he did not become a hero of faith, but he came to the borderline of faith. Calling his fate a test sent by God only strengthened his conviction that he was in the right and that this test must be a transitory thing.

And how does the story end? Note that the work we are examining deals with the problem of "repetition." Job was blessed, and everything was restored to him double. For him, then, there was a repetition; but it passed through a tempest in which Job was shown to be both in the right and in the wrong. He was in the wrong, "for he cannot appeal beyond the judgment seat that has condemned him." But he was also in the right "because he was in the wrong *before God*." Repetition and restoration came about for Job when all conceivable human certainty and probability argued that it was impossible, when hope had vanished bit by bit, when to the outward eye all was lost. In this moment God answers him from the whirlwind, bringing him down to utter humiliation and exalting him beyond measure.

Job's fate and that of the young man with his love story seem scarcely comparable in terms of the problems they pose; but this difference is not important for Kierkegaard's purpose in describing this experiment. The young man himself realizes this when he says to Job:

> I did not possess your riches, I did not have seven sons and three daughters. But even he who possessed little can lose everything; even he who lost the woman he loved can lose thereby both sons and daughters; and even he who lost his pride and honor, the strength and meaning of his life, has been smitten with sore boils.

At least in this point we must see Kierkegaard himself behind the pseudonymous young man. Here Kierkegaard, once more writing for himself as reader, is describing the problems of his own life.

In 1844 there appeared an "Edifying Discourse" on the subject "The Thorn in the Flesh"; it belongs together with the two works under discussion. We may recall that in these discourses, which he published under his own name in a constant stream to accompany his pseudonymous production, Kierkegaard seeks to present with his right hand that which the pseudonymous works present with the left. Here, without the distance established by the pseudonyms and without the cover of irony, Kierkegaard seeks to speak directly to "that individual" he is always searching for with these discourses, as he says over and over in the Foreword: "That individual whom I am pleased and grateful to call my reader." The discourse takes as its text 2 Corinthians 12:7, where the Apostle Paul, having told how he was caught up into the third heaven, adds, "And to keep me from being too elated by the abundance of revelations, a thorn was given me in the flesh, a messenger of Satan, to harass me, to keep me from being too elated."

We read in this discourse:

> If a man should die without ever having experienced what it means to strive with God, would this be a sign that he who lies buried was of

rare greatness in the fear of God? If he had never experienced what it means to be forsaken by God, would this be a sign that he who lies buried was a rare favorite of the Lord? If he had never experienced the wrath of the Lord and the Lord's consuming fire, if he had never even dreamed that such a thing existed, could that be his consolation at death, his justification at the judgment, a sign to him that he had been God's friend as no other man had ever been? Or could he give satisfaction by replying: I never had the chance to experience such a thing?

Then at least he should not try to explain what the "thorn in the flesh" meant to the Apostle.

As soon as he becomes aware of his suffering and the thorn begins to torment him, the Apostle is left to his own devices. His bliss has vanished, it retreats further and further into the distance. When present it was unspeakable; the misery, too, is unspeakable, since he cannot even speak of his loss, and in the memory of his bliss can only languish helplessly! To have been caught up into the third heaven, secure within the womb of bliss, extended in God—and now, with the thorn in the flesh, restricted to the slavery of earthly life! To have abounded in God, abounded indescribably—and now reduced to nothing, flesh and blood, dust and mortality! To have stood personally in God's presence, and now forsaken by God, forsaken by himself, with only a wretched, imbecilic memory for consolation! Hard enough for a man to experience human faithlessness—but to discover that in God, too, there is change, alternation of light and darkness, that there is an angel of Satan who has power to banish a man from bliss! Where is there security for a man if not in the third heaven! But no, no, let us not go astray; we are now speaking as the world speaks, the world of those that do not know whereof they speak, who bear witness only to what they have experienced, but do not know how to speak humbly like an Apostle, submitting to God no matter what may come. The Apostle says that this change, too, is for his benefit. How simple and plain, how gentle, are his words! . . . To want to run more swiftly than ever and then be unable to move an inch; to want to purchase the moment by sacrificing all else and then to learn that the moment is not for sale, because "it is not a matter of what a man wants or how he runs, but only of God's mercy." That this can be of benefit to a man—who can understand it? Here the frivolous mind will not venture to help out with its usual explanation of what is beneficial in life.

And now the conclusion of the discourse:

> We have spoken of the thorn in the flesh; we have tried to give a universal explanation of the expression, that is, an explanation in terms that concern all men because they concern a single individual. In particular, we have not worried about what concrete meaning this expression may have had for Paul personally. Least of all was it our desire to inquire about its meaning as though asking whether Paul was great or small of stature, fair of face, etc. In particular, we do not want to attempt to suggest the specific thing, perhaps accidental, perhaps insignificant, that the thorn in the flesh can be for a particular individual . . . The universal explanation is this: the noblest of lives also has its suffering, indeed the most terrible suffering; no one must wish for something whose danger he deceitfully passes over; no one must be restive when subjected to dangers of which he may never have dreamed; no one must blindly praise the easy and comfortable days of his life. Let a man merely be alert to this risk—he is already on the point of beginning to fight the good fight. Consolation will come; but it must not be grasped too early. The author of this discourse is still young; he will not prevent anyone from being alarmed, for he will be unable to console anyone with the equivocal explanation that long life has taught him that the danger was not so great as the Apostle paints it and as every sensitive person has probably suspected it to be in his youth—until the ways part: the one fights the good fight of danger and fear; the other becomes prudent and rejoices blindly in his carefree life.

Dread and Sin

The moralist demands that each individual realize a universal goal. As we have seen, a man encounters this demand within the framework of his present fate, with which he must come to terms. But he encounters it in a form that already bears the stamp of a specific life, a fact which may place considerable obstacles in the way of his realization of the universal. In any case, a man's past history imposes a burden on him that prevents him from making a completely fresh start at any moment in his life. The open possibility of what he may become in the future is always restricted by what he has already become in the past. When a man begins to grasp this fact, he will be seized with dread, not knowing whether in the future any possibility at all is open to him that has not already been closed by the past.

When this happens, a man must take into account much more than his own past life; for his life does not begin with him: it is already burdened by the past of all his ancestors. It would avail him nothing to deceive himself on this point. He could of course try to claim responsibility only for his own personal life story and the guilt he has personally brought upon himself, but not that of his ancestors. But the moralist has already dealt with this attempt in Part II of *Either/Or:*

> The greater the freedom, the greater the guilt. It is the blessed mystery of the highest kind of freedom to assume hereditary guilt. Whoever is unwilling to do so is, if not a coward, at least craven; though perhaps not base, at least not high-minded.

This is a position shared, in such radical form, only by Nietzsche in the nineteenth century. Behind it we can glimpse once more the personal interests of Kierkegaard's own life. Not only did he inherit his melancholy from his father; he also felt himself compelled to assume that his father's conduct had brought God's curse upon the entire family, a God "visiting the iniquity of the fathers upon the children unto the third and fourth generation." This conviction obliterates the boundary not only between individual and hereditary guilt, but also between guilt and sickness. For Kierkegaard, it made the task of coming to terms with his own past and making it transparent through repentance as difficult as possible.

In this context, the phenomenon of *dread* comes into being, which Kierkegaard discussed in 1844 in *The Concept of Dread: a Simple Study Approaching the Theological Problem of Original Sin from the Direction of Psychology, by Vigilius Haufniensis.* Among the pseudonymous works, this book constitutes a kind of exception, in that, as Kierkegaard himself said, the author "speaks directly and even lectures a little." He added, "The somewhat academic form of this work is probably to blame for the favor it enjoyed, rather more than the other pseudonymous works, in the eyes of the academic community." This holds true not only for his time, but probably even more for our own. The "existentialists" of today are especially concerned with the phenomenon of dread. Heidegger, too, treats this work as an exception among the pseudonymous works because he considers it especially illuminating with regard to the existential structure of existence (*Dasein*). It is therefore important to note how Kierkegaard continued the passage in which he reported the approbation of the academic community: "I cannot deny that I think this favor is a misunderstanding." Why he said this, the contents of the work will show.

Viewed psychologically, dread, which must be carefully distinguished from fear and similar emotional states, is a "characteristic of the dreaming spirit." It has no specific object; we may speak of people who "dread the unknown." It is rather "the reality of freedom as possibility confronted by possibility." It is "sympathetic antipathy and antipathetic sympathy"; once again, we may speak of an "exquisite dread," an "uncommon, singular dread," etc. The author uses the Genesis account of the fall of man to illustrate how dread makes its appearance in a man. Instead of the unknown, dread was clothed in the form of an enigmatic statement: "but of the tree of the knowledge of good and evil you shall not eat, for in the day that you eat of it you shall die." Adam in his state of innocence cannot understand this statement: he has no idea what "good and evil" is. The prohibition only increases his dread of the unknown, because there is now an additional unknown: "the dreadful possibility of *power*." The same holds true for the threat of death. Once more, it is something Adam cannot understand; it only evokes for him the notion of something terrible.

> The infinite possibility of power awakened by the prohibition now comes even closer: this possibility points to a further possibility as its consequence. Thus innocence is driven to its last extremity. It is seized by dread in its relationship to what has been forbidden and to the consequent punishment. Innocence is not guilty; but yet a dread fills it as though it were already lost.

So far can psychology come in explaining dread, but no further.

The resulting fall of man is no longer susceptible to explanation by psychology. No science can answer the question of how sin came into the world; any attempt yields only the most ridiculous answers.

> It is now six thousand years since sin came into the world; men say this the same way they say it is now two thousand years since Nebuchadnezzar was turned into an ox. If this question is put in this fashion, no wonder the explanation does not follow . . . How sin came into the world is something that each individual understands in his own heart; if he seeks to learn it from someone else, it is a sure sign that he does not understand the problem.

The question of the origin of sin involves both the life history of the individual and the history of mankind. Two questions must be answered: how did sin come to infect the human race, and how does the particular individual come to share in the sinfulness of mankind? These two questions constitute the problem of *original sin*.

If we see in Adam the beginning of the human race, then the first question is: how did Adam become a sinner? In answering this question, it is absolutely essential not to explain Adam's sin in a way that sets Adam so far apart from mankind as to make it impossible later to establish a connection between the sin of other men and the sin of Adam. This criterion immediately excludes two attempted explanations that play a significant role in the history of theology. The Roman Catholic doctrine of Adam's original state accords him a *donum divinitus datum supernaturale,* a supernatural divine endowment, which he then loses at the fall. This theory fails to look upon Adam as a man like any other, and therefore his fall can have no significance for succeeding generations. There is equally little to gain from the fantastic theory that views Adam merely as the representative of mankind. "Naturally neither explanation can explain anything, since the one only explains away its own invention, and the other only invents something that explains nothing."

Any explanation of original sin is false if it suggests that a man coming afterward participates in original sin only through his relationship to Adam and not through a primitive relationship to sin. This means that Adam's sin, if it is to explain original sin, must be explained in such a way that sin in succeeding generations can arise in essentially the same manner. What explains Adam must also explain the human race, and vice versa. This is due to the relationship of every individual to the race. "Man is an individual and, as such, both a unique self and the entire race, so that the entire race participates in the individual and the individual in the entire race." This antithesis determines the task of the individual; the movement produced by this task determines his life history. If the individual is both a unique self and also the human race, then the history of the human race progresses continuously, while the particular individual constantly begins anew with the history of the human race. Adam, too, is both a unique self and the human race; therefore what explains him must also explain the human race, and vice versa.

The task of explaining Adam's sin consists in explaining his first sin. Sinfulness as a human quality does not come about as the sum total of particular sins, and the first sin has more than numerical signifiance as the chance beginning of a series of particular sins. "The first sin defines a new quality; the first sin is sin itself." How, then, did this first sin come into the world? It cannot have happened by accident, since no accident can disturb the order of creation. Neither can the cause have been something necessary, since this would mean that creation would bear within itself the necessity for its own destruction. There can be only one place for sin to enter: it must presuppose itself. It is simply there the moment the quality establishes itself. This contradiction is the only dialectically consistent interpretation; it is contained in the Genesis narrative, and all its meaning is concentrated in one sentence: *Sin came into the world through sin.*

If we call the condition of man before sin *innocence,* the explanation of the fall of man must also explain how he lost his innocence. Innocence is lost not through innocence, but only through guilt. Neither can it be neutralized by a motion of immanent logic and transformed into guilt. This would violate the border of logic, and ethics would have to protest. The transition from innocence to guilt is a transformation of qualities, which can be explained only by that leap with which the new quality of sin establishes itself. In other words, the ultimate explanation is simply to assume that postulate, as dogmatic theology does in the case of original sin. Every attempted explanation, if it is correct, must finally have recourse to this postulate. Not even dogmatic theology can explain original sin. "It explains original sin by postulating it, just like the whirl that the natural philosophy of the Greeks describes as a moving something that no science can grasp." Psychology can push its explanation to the point of the leap and afterward explain the consequences of the leap, but for the leap itself psychology must turn to dogmatics. This limitation must be strictly observed whenever psychology at least attempts to explain as much as is actually possible. If, for example, one seeks to explain the fall of man (as frequently happens) by suggesting that the prohibition aroused *concupiscentia,* longing, then psychology is being asked to perform beyond its competence. *Concupiscentia* is itself a definition of sin and guilt, and so cannot explain their origin. To introduce *concupiscentia* as a middle term between guilt and innocence is to substitute for a qualitative leap a quantitative transition that completely effaces both concepts.

The Genesis narrative points the way to the proper explanation by defining innocence as ignorance. Man is a synthesis of body and soul, united in the spirit as the third element. In the state of innocence the spirit is present, but turns out to be a nothing as soon as one seeks to apprehend it. "In a dream, the spirit projects its own reality; but this reality is a nothing; but this nothing constantly beholds innocence." And this nothing gives rise to dread, in which man becomes guilty. If one seeks to explain further how this equivocal state of innocence caught up in dread changes into guilt, the explanation must be equally equivocal:

> . . . whoever becomes guilty through dread is nevertheless innocent: it was not he himself, but dread, an alien force that seized him, a force that he did not love, but rather dreaded—and yet he is guilty, for the dread that he loved by fearing it has swallowed him up.

This ambiguity proves that the explanation is psychologically correct; for there is no other way to explain the doctrine of original sin, which declares that sin establishes itself by its own power.

Now if what explains Adam's sin is also to explain the sin of an individual follower of Adam, one must assume that every man once possessed innocence; otherwise he could not become guilty. The history of the human race's sinfulness cannot therefore be summed up by saying that the qualitative leap was accomplished in Adam's sin for all those yet to come. Each individual must accomplish this leap himself. The difference between Adam and those who follow after him is not qualitative but quantitative: it lies in the natural tendency to sinfulness that precedes the qualitative leap. But wherein does this heightened predisposition to sin consist? The consequence of Adam's sin was twofold: ". . . that sin came into the world and that sexuality was established, without any way to separate the one from the other." Before the fall, sexual differentiation existed only in ignorance; in other words, it had no real existence. In human beings, it can never be completely instinctive, as it is in animals, neither before nor after the fall, because man is a synthesis sustained by spirit. "The moment the spirit establishes itself it establishes the synthesis; but in order to establish the synthesis it must first penetrate it and separate it; and sexuality is the ultimate expression of man's sensuality." Prior to this moment, the individual is actually neither animal nor man. When the spirit establishes itself the individual becomes man by simultaneously becoming animal. Sensuality and its ultimate expression, sexuality, are therefore not themselves identical with sinfulness; but without sin there would be no sexuality. Without sexuality, however, there would be no history. Perfect spirit, which we shall be in the resurrection, therefore possesses neither the one nor the other. "Only in sexuality is the synthesis established as an antithesis. At the same time, like every antithesis, it becomes a task, whose historical performance begins in the same instant." This history is the reality of freedom, but it is preceded by the possibility of freedom. This possibility within the man who possesses sexuality in ignorance is not, however, the possibility of choosing good or evil, but once more only the possibility of power. And this possibility once more gives rise to dread. The possession of sexuality, in other words, does not itself make man sinful; sexuality only gives rise to the dread that must lead to the qualitative leap by which man becomes guilty in essentially the same way as Adam. Even though sexuality was raised to the level of consciousness through Adam's sin, it does not automatically have the same significance for the next individual that it had for Adam after the fall. Each individual begins all over again with sexual innocence, only to lose it in essentially the same way as Adam. The history of the human race's sinfulness can be summed up merely by saying that unconscious sexuality produces in the individual follower of Adam a quantitative increase in dread, strengthening the tendency toward the qualitative leap.

In the individual follower of Adam dread is more clearly defined than in Adam. This is because the object of dread gradually ceases to be an unknown nothing and becomes a something. The unknown nothing of dread takes shape as a complex of mutually reinforcing misgivings that increase the individual's dread at an accelerating rate. But it must be remembered that this nothing counts as something only when considered psychologically. The individual in a state of innocence can never become guilty by himself through this increase in dread. "This something, which is original sin *stricte sic dicta,* is primarily the *result of the generative relationship.*" The beginning of this relationship can already be seen in the relationship between Adam and Eve. Eve was not created primitively; she was created out of Adam. She is therefore a derived being, not as primitive as Adam.

> Of course she is innocent, like Adam; but there is something like a presentiment of a tendency, which is not really present but can appear as a hint of the sinfulness established by propagation. This is the derived element that gives the individual a predisposition but does not make him guilty.

Scripture says that Eve is tempted first; this indicates that the predisposition to sin (i.e., dread) was already greater in her than in Adam, precisely because she was no longer perfectly primitive. Essentially, of course, Eve, like all succeeding generations, was as primitive as Adam. But the way Eve came into being shows metaphorically the results of the generative relationship, which creates a quantitative difference between Adam and his followers. "For all subsequent individuals, the difference, *in pleno,* is that they are derived; for each individual, however, this difference can be positive or negative."

The fact of being derived means an increase in sensuality. As sensuality increases through the process of generation, so also does dread. Every individual has behind him the human race's history, into which he is born. Within this history of the human race sinfulness has its history. The individual enters into this history, in which the sins of the fathers are visited upon the children.

> This increase of dread and sensuality that each subsequent individual has with respect to Adam can of course be a positive or negative quantity in each particular individual. Here there are differences so terrible in reality that certainly no one would dare reflect on them in the deeper sense, i.e., with genuine human sympathy, unless he had previously assured himself with unshakable certainty that the world has never witnessed, nor ever will, such an increase that would transform a quantitative difference into a qualitative difference through a simple transition.

The problems of Kierkegaard's own life stand out with particular clarity behind this passage. At this crucial point in the author's argument, we can observe the passion with which the problem of original sin has been worked out. There is room here for the most terrible burden imposed by the life history of one's forefathers, where inherited sensuality can maximize the dread within the spirit, which is to incorporate sensuality into its synthesis. At this point dread of sin and dread of sin's inescapability become so intense that sin generates itself. But even at this maximum limit of dread one fact remains unshakably certain: in no case can dread be transformed into sin necessarily and of its own accord, that is, without the individual himself accomplishing this leap into sin through his own first sin.

The individual shares in the history of the human race not only through his own personal inheritance but also through living in a human environment. The increase of dread, original sin, is therefore due to more than the effect of the generative relationship; it is also a *consequence of the historical relationship*. The individual has a historical environment in which it becomes evident that sensuality can mean sinfulness. This in turn increases dread in the individual. The maximum this dread can reach—corresponding to the maximum in the generative relationship—is for the individual, in dread of being considered guilty, to become guilty by committing a sin.

Let us turn our gaze backward for a moment:

> If man were an animal or an angel, he could not be in dread. He is,
> though, a synthesis of body and soul, established through spirit. Be-
> cause it is his duty to accomplish this synthesis, he can be in dread; and
> the more he is in dread, the greater he is.

Dread has nothing to do with fear of any terrors life may hold. Unlike
fear, it does not grow out of a relationship to anything finite. It is associated with the possibility of freedom, since it consumes everything
finite, exposing all illusions in what it consumes. Therefore, only dread
can discipline man absolutely. Now of course there are men who boast
that they never experience dread. The author says:

> To this I would reply that of course no one should be in dread of
> men, of anything finite. But only he who has passed through the
> dread of possibility is so trained that he has ceased to be in dread, not
> because he escapes the terrors of life, but because he finds them all too
> feeble in comparison with the terrors of possibility. Should the speaker
> suggest, on the contrary, that what makes him great is his never hav-
> ing experienced dread, I would be delighted to disclose my explanation
> of this phenomenon to him, namely, that he is quite devoid of spirit.

The crucial question of course remains: how can a man trained by this
dread find a way out and not become lost? In answering this question,
Kierkegaard parts company completely with modern "existentialists" of
all schools; he would have no more toleration for their recognition than
he had for the favor of the "academic community," which he considered
a misunderstanding. For Kierkegaard, there is no possibility for dread
somehow to transform itself into freedom, for man to escape from dread
by his own efforts. In order to escape, man must have faith, which alone
can overcome dread. Dread disciplines and trains man absolutely, as
we have seen; but this is true only when it is associated with faith. To
expose oneself to dread without faith is to venture into mortal danger.
Therefore Kierkegaard has his Vigilius Haufniensis say:

> I will not deny it. Whoever is disciplined and trained through possibility
> is not exposed to the danger that confronts those that are disciplined
> and trained by things that are finite, the danger of falling among bad
> company and erring somehow from the way. But to one danger he
> is exposed, suicide. If, at the beginning of his training, he misunder-

stands dread, so that it guides him not toward but away from faith, he is lost. The man who is properly trained, however, remains steadfast in dread; he refuses to be deceived by its innumerable guiles; he scrupulously retains his memory of the past. The onset of dread remains terrible, but it can no longer drive him to flight. Dread becomes a ministering spirit, which, against its will, must guide him wherever he wishes. When it announces its presence, when it cunningly pretends to have discovered completely new terrors, acting more terrible than ever, he does not retreat; still less does he attempt to hold dread at bay with alarms and excursions. Instead he welcomes it, he greets it ceremoniously, as Socrates ceremoniously drained the cup of hemlock. He draws it to himself and says, like a patient to the surgeon when the painful operation is to begin, "Now I am ready." Then dread penetrates his soul; it searches out everything; it puts to flight everything within him that is finite and trivial, and then guides him wherever he wishes.

To this faith that overcomes dread we must now turn our attention.

Sin and Faith

Man is a synthesis of soul and body, established by spirit, the third element. We have already examined this synthesis from the point of view of the resultant dread. Now we must examine it from the point of view of *despair*. But first one remark by way of preface.

You have no doubt noticed that it is not particularly easy to follow Kierkegaard's train of thought. This is hardly remarkable, since he is dealing with difficult problems, the analysis of which demands considerable effort. But this difficulty is not really intellectual. We shall now discuss *The Sickness unto Death: a Christiano-psychological Treatise for Edification and Revival, by Johannes Anti-Climacus, edited by Søren Kierkegaard,* 1849. Kierkegaard says of it, "This small work is in *one* sense so constituted that a seminarian could write it; in another sense, though, it is so constituted that not all professors could write it." What does he mean by this?

He means that this work discusses problems that cannot be disposed of in the usual academic way, but must be reflected upon and discussed in a way that serves for "edification," as we read in the subtitle of the work: ". . . for edification and revival." And he goes on to say in the Foreword:

> The scientific approach, which is not ultimately edifying as well, is for this very reason unchristian. Everything Christian must share something in its presentation with the statements of the physician at the sickbed; though only the doctor may understand them, one must never forget that the statements are made beside the sickbed. This relationship of Christianity to life (in contrast to a scientific detachment from life), or this ethical side of Christianity, is precisely what is edifying. This manner of presentation, however rigorous it may be, is totally different,

qualitatively different, from the scientific manner. The scientific manner remains indifferent; its exalted heroism is, by Christian standards, so far from being heroism that it appears to the Christian eye as a kind of inhuman curiosity.

This time, too, you will have to exert a real effort to follow Kierkegaard's train of thought, which remains exceptionally rigorous in its dialectical precision. I hope you will discover, however, that you have not done so for the sake of inhuman scientific precision, but that man is always the central concern.

The author begins with a precise definition of this man:

> Man is spirit. But what is spirit? Spirit is the self. But what is the self? The self is a relationship that is related to itself, or in the relationship that relates the relationship to itself. The self is not the relationship, but the aspect of the relationship by which the relationship is related to itself.

This definition of man, which must delight any dialectician by its concise clarity, must now be expanded in more detail. The self is a relationship because man is a synthesis of infinite and finite, of temporal and eternal, of freedom and necessity. But as long as man remains only a synthesis between two such antitheses, he is not yet a self. A third element is necessary to place the two opposites in a relationship, and this third element is the self, in which the relationship is related to itself.

And now the next step: "Such a relationship, which is related to itself, must either have established itself or have been established by something else." Here again Kierkegaard and most of the modern "existentialists" part company. Kierkegaard postulates that the self has not established itself but was established by something else, leaving open for a moment who or what this something else might be. If, however, the

> relationship related to itself is established by something else, then the relationship is certainly the third element; but this relationship, the third element, is once again a relationship, since it is related to whatever established the entire relationship.

The human self is therefore a *derived* relationship, that is, a relationship that, although admittedly related to itself, is in its relationship to itself also related to something else, by which it was established.

Now man can fail to fulfill his destiny and be a self by becoming sick in his spirit. This sickness in the spirit, in the self, the author calls *despair;* on the basis of his definition of man he works out the schema for the various possible forms of despair. The first form, which he calls "counterfeit despair," is present when "the human spirit in despair is ignorant that it possesses a self." Because the despairing man has no knowledge of his self, he is naturally ignorant of his despair in this case; but he nevertheless despairs. Therefore we are dealing here with "counterfeit" despair. The second form, despair "proper," has two possibilities: *a*) man can "desperately seek not to be himself," seek to be rid of himself; and *b*) the exact opposite, man can "desperately seek to be himself," that is, to tear his self free from the power that established it. All these forms of despair have one thing in common: they represent a misunderstanding in the relationship in which the self is related to itself. At the same time, though, this improper relationship is reflected in the relationship to the power that established the relationship.

If man were "not a synthesis, he could not despair; and if God's hand had not originally established the synthesis in the proper relationship, he also could not despair." Now God, by making man into a relationship, also released man from his hand, in order that the relationship can be related to itself. Therefore this duty and possibility of "possessing a self, being a self, is the greatest boon that has been granted man, an infinite boon; but it is also a demand that eternity makes of him." In this distinction lies also the possibility of this sickness of despair, which marks man's superiority over the animals.

> And this superiority distinguishes him in a way far different from his upright posture, for it suggests infinite uprightness or nobility, it suggests that he is spirit. The possibility of this sickness is the superiority of man to the animals; to be alert to this sickness is the Christian's superiority to natural man; to be healed of this sickness is the Christian's bliss.

We may now ask in what sense despair is called a "sickness unto death." The author takes as his point of departure the story of the raising of Lazarus in the eleventh chapter of the Gospel of John. He asks why Jesus could say, "This illness is not unto death," although Lazarus was already dead. He answers: not because Lazarus was raised from the dead; that is not the reason one can say that *this* sickness is not unto death. Because He is there who is the resurrection and the life, that is why this sickness is not unto death.

> For humanly speaking death is the last of all things, and humanly speaking hope exists only so long as life is present. But the Christian understands that death is by no means the last of all things, that even death is only an unimportant event within an all-inclusive eternal life; and the Christian understands that in death there is infinitely more hope than where, humanly speaking, there is not only life, but life in fullest health and strength.

From the Christian point of view, then, death is not the "sickness unto death," let alone everything else in the world that is called suffering and misery and evil. To all this the Christian is superior. But in return Christianity discovered another form of misery otherwise unknown to man: the horror of despair. That is the "sickness unto death." One does not die of this sickness.

> On the contrary, the torture of despair is precisely the fact that one cannot die. It is therefore more like the condition of a man mortally ill, when he lies there striving with death and unable to die. Therefore to be sick *unto* death means to be unable to die—not as though there were still hope for life; no, there is no hope precisely because the final hope, death, does not exist. When death is the greatest danger, one hopes for life; but when one comes to know the still more terrible danger, one hopes for death. When the danger is so great that death becomes man's hope, despair is hopelessness, the loss of hope even for death. In this last sense despair is the sickness unto death, this agonizing contradiction, this sickness in the self, to die eternally, to die and yet not die, to die death. For dying means that it is past, but dying death means that one lives through the process of dying . . . Should a man die of despair as one dies of a sickness, the eternal element within him, the self, would have to be able to die in the same sense that the body dies of sickness. But that is impossible; dying of despair is constantly transformed into a kind of life. The desperate man cannot die. "No more than the dagger can kill thoughts" can despair consume the eternal element, the self, that lies behind despair, whose worm does not die and whose fire is not quenched.

Despair is helpless self-consumption. This very helplessness is

> what provokes, or it is the cold fire in despair, a corrosion that constantly creeps inward, going deeper and deeper into helpless self-con-

sumption . . . A man despairs because he cannot consume himself, cannot be freed of himself, cannot become nothing. That is the exponential formula for despair, the rising of the fever in this sickness of the self.

We shall now ask at once, without going into the individual stages and forms of this sickness in detail, how it can be *healed*. The author describes the condition in which despair is exorcised as follows: "In relating to itself and in seeking to be itself, the self becomes grounded transparently in the power that established it." How can the self come to the point of being healed of despair?

The intensification of the sickness proceeds from counterfeit, unconscious despair to conscious despair, despair proper. But if despair increases exponentially with the degree of consciousness, the question arises how far this increase can go. It is open to question

> to what extent a perfectly clear view of the self and perfect awareness that one is desperate can be reconciled with the state of despair, i.e., whether this clarity of recognition and self-awareness must not itself snatch a man out of his despair, make him so terrified of himself that he ceases to be desperate.

Part of this clarity about despair is the knowledge that it arises from something eternal. Would not this insight itself bring a man to reorder his relationship to the eternal? The demand imposed on the self to ground itself transparently in the power that established it means nothing less than a completely clear self-awareness, which at one glance takes in the whole double relationship of the self. Now if this absolute transparency is brought about, will not this insight of its own accord transform despair into faith? This would be the case if the relationship between proper insight and proper action were such, as Socrates, for example, taught, that no one knowing what is right could do what is wrong. Socrates, however, like every moralist, came up against the fact that action does not always immediately follow insight, that instead action is often blocked by that obstacle which can be called "sin." But this did not shake Socrates' basic confidence that this obstacle still arises from lack of insight. "What is lacking in Socrates' definition of sin?" asks the author. He replies:

> The will, defiance! The Greek intellect was too happy, too naïve, too aesthetic, too ironic, too witty—in short, too sinful, to grasp the pos-

sibility that someone might deliberately refuse to do the good or deliberately, consciously, do wrong. Graciousness establishes an intellectual categorical imperative.

Therefore the man immersed in the Greek way of thinking can think of sin only in Socratic terms, that is, he cannot think otherwise than that he is continuously approaching the self that he is to become. Because he has no other criterion than his own human self, he can never hit upon the idea that this self is still a quality too deep. And because he has not the slightest idea of a qualitative difference, he can naturally never hit upon the idea that this difference is sin. "No man of himself can say what sin is, precisely because he is in sin." If man is to know this, he must first have come to know it from God through a revelation. One can know what sin is only "after one has been enlightened about what sin is by a revelation: in despair before God to seek to be oneself or in despair to seek not to be oneself."

It is extremely important for Kierkegaard that the religion of immanence may know what guilt is, but not what sin is.

> The concept that distinguishes Christianity qualitatively most absolutely from paganism is sin, the doctrine of sin. Therefore Christianity quite logically assumes that neither paganism nor natural man knows what sin is, assumes, in fact, that a revelation from God is needed to reveal what sin is. The assumption made by superficial observation is not true, namely, that the doctrine of the atonement constitutes the qualitative difference between paganism and Christianity. No, one must begin much deeper, with sin, with the doctrine of sin, as Christianity itself does. What a dangerous objection to Christianity it would be if paganism had a definition of sin that Christianity had to recognize as correct.

But the Christian doctrine of sin also differs at another point from the Socratic or any other natural explanation of sin. For Socrates, sin is a negation, whereas Christianity declares it to be something *positive*.

> Orthodox theology and orthodoxy have constantly battled for the truth of this position and rejected as pantheistic any definition of sin that makes it out to be something merely negative: weakness, sensuality, finitude, ignorance, or the like. Orthodoxy has seen quite rightly that this is where the battle must be fought.

This is extremely important for our inquiry into how the healing of the

sickness of despair is to proceed. The condition in which despair is exorcised is *faith*. "Faith is the self's grounding itself transparently in God by
being itself and seeking to be itself." Virtue is therefore by no means the
opposite of sin, as is commonly supposed.

> No, the opposite of sin is faith; therefore we read in Romans 14:23,
> "whatever does not proceed from faith is sin." And this is among the
> most crucial statements of all Christianity, that the opposite of sin is
> not virtue, but faith.

The road from the sickness of despair to its conquest through faith leads,
as we have seen, through a constantly increasing awareness on the part of
man that he is in despair. In this increase of self-awareness, which leads
to ever increasing transparency, the self comes upon sin. After man has
come to know what sin is through revelation, he must absorb this
knowledge into his self-awareness, that is, he must "become transparent
to himself as a sinner." But how is this position of sin eliminated?
This also takes place through revelation, which, at the same time it gives
knowledge of sin, also provides the possibility of forgiveness of sin.

> First Christianity goes and establishes the position of sin so securely
> that human understanding can never comprehend it; then it is this same
> Christian doctrine that takes it upon itself to eliminate this position
> so completely that human understanding can never comprehend it.

Just as the Christian revelation reveals sin to be disobedience toward
God, so it also makes abiding in sin an additional act of disobedience.
When God offers man the forgiveness of sins, an imperative lurks behind the offer: "You must, *you must* believe in the forgiveness of sins."
Now the self no longer has merely God as its standard; it receives once
more an exponential increase through the knowledge of Christ. Only
through Christ does the self really come to have God as its standard;
without Christ it lacks the proper conception of God. At this point, however, the stress this standard places on the self is increased immensely
by the knowledge "that for the guilt of this self God suffered himself to
be born, became man, and died." The new increase of sin in this self
that has Christ as its standard is *"the sin of despairing of the forgiveness
of sin."* This form of despair, too, can be reduced to the two forms that
recur in all kinds of despair: despair based on weakness and despair
based on defiance. But here defiance and weakness exchange roles.

Formerly it was weakness to seek desperately not to be one's self. Here it is defiance; it is defiance to seek not to be what one is, a sinner, and thereby dispense with the forgiveness of sins. Previously it was defiance to seek desperately to be oneself. Here it is weakness to seek so strongly to be oneself, a sinner, that there can be no forgiveness.

Now we appear to have reached the ultimate degree of despair in sin: the sin of refusing to have faith in the forgiveness of sins and so remaining in despair. But there still remains a final increment of despair in sin. We must note that the revelation intended to make man recognize himself as a sinner and have faith in the forgiveness of his sin is not something that a man can simply accept intellectually in order to cross over from sin to faith. Instead, this revelation encounters him as a paradox that challenges not only a man's intellect, but his entire existence. The revelation that tells of sin and the forgiveness of sins is therefore not simply a doctrine that can be accepted on its face; it always involves the possibility that the man to whom it comes will not believe it, but instead be offended by it. This possibility of offense is, in fact, a necessary part of every item of revealed knowledge, so that the man to whom it is revealed must involve his entire existence in his decision for faith, rejecting the offense. If this constant possibility of offense were removed, the final step from sin to faith would be a thoroughly human possibility. Sin would cease to be a position, the qualitative difference between God and man would be abolished, and the whole doctrine of the incarnate God would become a pantheistic paganism and would lead, from the Christian point of view, to blasphemy.

Faith is never reached, therefore, except by way of the possibility of offense. Now we come to the final possible degree of despair in sin. It consists in a man's refusing either to take offense at the revelation or to have faith in it, and instead denying it the very right to confront him with the decision between offense and faith. "That is the *sin against the Holy Spirit*. Here the self has reached the ultimate degree of despair. Not only does it reject Christianity entire, it makes Christianity out to be a lie and a fraud." The man simply steps out of the circle that revelation would draw about him, refusing even to acknowledge its demands. Now sin takes the offensive against God. "Everything that went before at least somehow acknowledged that its opponent was the stronger. Now, however, sin turns to the attack." This "sin against the Holy

Spirit is the positive form of taking offense." It no longer resists, but simply surrenders Christianity *modo ponendo*. And it is quite consistent that this final form of despair, which is now really incurable, is not recognized as such. As the author says, "It is usually overlooked since the Christian antithesis between sin and faith is not accepted."

If we now look back and review this entire train of thought, it becomes clear that Kierkegaard's thought does not move in a straight line from the natural to the Christian, but rather in a circle, which must constantly return to its point of departure. Kierkegaard is always thinking with the Christian imperative at his back, even when in the first instance he speaks in purely human terms. Only in this way can he come to see this final form of despair as the most desperate form of human self-assertion and condemn it. Obviously one could not speak of despair under these conditions except by the presupposition of Christianity. To Kierkegaard, however, this form of despair is ultimate apostasy from the spirit, because it denies the very presupposition behind the existence of spirit.

> It declares Christianity a lie and a fraud; it denies Christ (that he existed and that he was who he claimed to be) either docetically or rationalistically, so that Christ either ceases to be a particular individual, being only an apparition, or else becomes only a particular individual. Christ becomes docetically mere poetry and mythology without any claim to reality, or rationalistically a reality without any claim to divinity. In this denial of Christ the paradox once more involves the denial of everything Christian: sin, the forgiveness of sin, etc.

Because it abolishes Christianity, the presupposition behind all forms of spiritual existence, it is the "sin against the Holy Spirit."

The Dialectic of Existence

We may remember that Kierkegaard considered his life's goal to be the introduction of Christianity into Christendom. We may recall also that he thought he had to do this in a situation in which this Christianity, with the aid of Hegel's philosophy, thought it had emerged victorious from the great battle with the Enlightenment. The Christian revelation had merged into a synthesis with all of human history, both political and intellectual, whose grandeur can scarcely be equaled by anything else in the entire history of the church. The only comparable achievement was that of Thomas Aquinas, on the Roman Catholic side. If Kierkegaard had not been sensitive to the greatness of this conception, if it had not represented even for him a temptation not without danger, he would not have attacked it so passionately as the mortal enemy of everything Christian. Why did he think this was necessary?

Today Hegel's philosophy is valued differently than it was then. Ever since Marxism laid claim to it, albeit with a basic modification of its principles, the greatness and boldness of its conception have become suspect. It can therefore hardly be a real temptation to any of us. To this extent, it might appear that Kierkegaard's whole attack upon Hegel was only an ephemeral incident that has lost its significance for us. To think this, however, would be a mistake, in part because it is impossible in the history of philosophy, as in other kinds of history, to simply skip over an epoch with impunity. It is by no means settled that Hegel's philosophy will not some day experience a joyful resurrection outside the realm of Marxism. Even if this should prove not to be the case, Hegel nevertheless represents a break and a turning point in the history of philosophical problems, a turning point that will have its effects even where one may think it can be ignored. Therefore the question why Kierkegaard thought it necessary to attack Hegel's philosophy with such passion remains as relevant today as it was then.

As we said earlier, Kierkegaard objected to Hegel primarily on the grounds that the latter's philosophy was dishonest, that he had evaded the central question and set his dialectic in motion by a trick. An entry in Kierkegaard's *Journal* reads:

> If one attempts to characterize the confusion of modern philosophy in brief, in a single word, particularly since the time that, to use a cliché, it forsook Kant's "honest course" and, if I may put it so, squandered the proverbial hundred talers in order to become theocentric, I know of no better word to describe it than "dishonest."

Kierkegaard is here referring to Kant's refutation of the ontological proof of God's existence propounded by Anselm of Canterbury. This proof argues from the concept of a highest being to the reality of such a being in this fashion: when the concept of a most perfect being is formed, this being has its existence first of all as the intellectual content of the mind (*esse in intellectu*). If it did not at the same time exist in reality (*esse etiam in re*), it would not be the most perfect being, since a higher being could then be conceived that existed not only in the mind but also at the same time in reality. Therefore the concept of God as the most perfect being implies at once his reality. Anselm himself constructs the proof on the presupposition of the Christian revelation. It is philosophically convincing only on the presupposition that being can be conceived only in the actual state of being, i.e., that thought possesses reality. Kant's critique of reason cast doubt on this presupposition. In his refutation of the ontological proof, Kant shows that conceptually there is no difference between a hundred possible talers and a hundred real talers, but that there is a difference as regards their reality. He says:

> Therefore the famous ontological proof of the existence of a supreme being on the basis of concepts is nothing but wasted effort; a man can no more become richer in insights by means of mere ideas than a merchant can increase his wealth by adding a few zeroes to the contents of his till in order to better his position.

Now to what extent did Hegel forsake Kant's "honest course" and, as Kierkegaard puts it, squander those hundred talers? Kant had devoted much thought to the relationship between thought and being, and had come to the conclusion that their correspondence is something *an sich,* "in itself," that continually evades the thought process. Kant's Idealistic successors saw in this *Ding an sich,* "thing in itself," the weakness of his system. By its means Kant had sought to retain a remnant of objectivity external to the subject, but at the cost, as one man put it, that without the *Ding an sich* there is no entering Kant's philosophy and with it there is no staying there. It was the young Fichte who pointed a new way by discarding the entire question of an objectivity external to the subject as the object of knowledge and seeking in the subject itself what exists *an sich.* The whole epistemological process now takes place within the ego, which, as the producing ego, is identical with the produced ego. Within this abstract identity of the ego with itself, absolute idealism, with only the subject as its point of departure, sought to solve the epistemological problem. This course, following the young Fichte, was that taken not only by Hegel, but by Kierkegaard himself. But despite this common starting point their ways diverge completely at the problem which arises once more: reality.

With this radical turn of attention to the subject, all the fundamental concepts of epistemology had lost the meaning they had had in the period from Descartes to Kant. After the object that transcends consciousness had fallen, the subject-object problem had to take on a basically different meaning. Now that thought has itself as its object, the place of doubt in the old image scheme is taken by self-reflection. This self-reflection could of course give rise to a system of reason within self-awareness; but now what had formerly been called the objective character of knowledge must become the most acute problem. The consistent Idealists had given up the *Ding an sich;* but now how were they to solve the problem of *reality?* This is the point upon which all Kierkegaard's interest in Idealistic philosophy focuses; and this is the point at which he collides with Hegel.

Hegel rejects the Kantian distinction between knowledge and the *Ding an sich,* between "I" and "not-I," seeking reality within the thinking ego itself. The reality of thought, which had been presupposed in the Middle Ages and called in question by Kant, is now restored by a movement of thought within itself. Hegel is confident that, in the act of thinking, what is thought and thought itself are equivalent. And this self-confidence of the thinking individual is confidence in the spirit, in which thought itself and what is thought are identical, and which in turn brings it about that between the thinking self and the spirit the same identity exists as between what is thought and thought itself. Moreover, the ultimate ground of this identity is the fact that the spirit is equated with God, so that in my thinking of the absolute the absolute thinks of itself. All this is comprehensible only if one realizes clearly that this thinking is an act, a process, that the concepts used in thinking do not describe a state, but rather an event: the event in which God, the absolute spirit, is constantly at work. The process of thought does not produce a statistically ascertainable relationship of reason within what is thought; in the act of thinking, reason becomes an event. What is thought is not a state; thought is a living process of becoming. The reality of our thinking is a component of the reality of God, who cannot be thought of statically, but only in his continual activity of creation and revelation. Because human thinking is identical with the event of reason or the idea of the spirit, because the reality brought about by this thinking is identical with the reality of God, this thinking is the *pure* thinking, free from all the random accidents of history, in which the absolute spirit thinks of itself. This is what Kierkegaard means when he says that this thinking has become "theocentric."

But what is actually the *object* of this pure thinking? Here we must free ourselves of all our traditional ideas of thinking according to the subject-object schema, where the thinking individual confronts an object of which he must form an image. The object of thinking is here the thinking individual himself in his act of thinking, through which he comprehends reality by creating it intellectually. This reality is not only the reality of his own personal ego, but also the reality of the entire history within which this ego lives and within which the absolute reason of the universe realizes itself. We can put it this way: the object of this thinking is historical life in its full breadth and depth, thought of as the life of reason, of the spirit, as the life of eternal, absolute truth. Thus what is reasonable becomes historical and, conversely, all history becomes reasonable. The result of this thinking is an all-inclusive system of truth. But this system itself must not be understood as an intellectual construction abstracted from life, which describes the reasonableness of the world as a state; the system is the rhythm of life itself, which realizes itself in the process of thinking.

According to the famous dialectical method, this process moves from thesis through antithesis to synthesis. This triad makes its influence felt everywhere. It shows up in the course of history, where every phenomenon moves toward its opposite, only to end in a *tertium quid* that constitutes the higher unity between the two opposites. This synthesis itself then becomes the starting point for a new dialectical movement. In this continual cycle of thesis, antithesis, and synthesis, the latter becoming once more a new thesis, the idea realizes itself in history, and the history of the world becomes the judgment of the world. The same triad appears in logic, where every concept produces its opposite, not, as by the principle of contradiction formerly held valid in logic, in order to exclude it, but rather to set it free as a necessary component of the original concept. The principle of contradiction is invalidated, since every concept turns into its opposite and both are then absorbed into a third, higher concept, which mediates between the two. All that matters is that the method remain in progress, that man not stand still in the one-sidedness of a particular thesis, thereby becoming trapped in error, lie, and sin. This method permits the resolution of all oppositions between thinking and being, between subject and object, between thing and idea, between nature and spirit, reconciling all in a higher unity. As soon as Hegel succeeds in setting this all-powerful method in motion, nothing can hold him.

But this is precisely Kierkegaard's question: how does this movement of pure thinking within itself actually begin, how is it set in motion? He says, "If the Hegelian philosophy is free from all postulates, it has achieved this result by means of one mad postulate, by the beginning of pure thinking." No more than the method can be set in motion can it be brought to a halt. Kierkegaard demonstrates this fact in his attacks upon Hegel's central concept of mediation, the middle term intended to link two concepts. Kierkegaard sees here that Hegel is simply weaseling, because he cannot answer the question: "How does the mediation come about? Does it result from an effort to join up on the part of the two components? Is it contained in them a priori? Does it come as something new?" According to Kierkegaard, Hegel is unable to answer these questions because he disregards the limits of logic and smuggles the notion of "becoming" into it. "In logic, no movement *becomes;* logic and everything logical can merely *be;* and just this impotence of what is logical is the transition of logic to becoming, where existence and reality appear." In all Kierkegaard's polemic against Hegel the same thought recurs again and again: Hegel cannot unify thinking and being. However much Hegel may desire it, pure thinking does not possess the category of reality in its concepts; it is an abstraction from reality. This is because the method can be set in motion only by an error, and can be kept in motion only by the same error. Hegel can maintain this error only by disregarding concrete reality in favor of being and reality as abstract concepts. This brings us to the decisive question already implied in all Kierkegaard's objections hitherto: how is the empirical subject of the thinking individual to transform himself into the subject of pure thinking so as to enter into the movement of the absolute spirit? Of what use is the most magnificent system if the thinker has forgotten the most important point: to include himself as a concrete individual with his own existence?

The course taken by Kierkegaard in his own existential dialectic is determined throughout by this opposition to Hegel. Both have the same starting point: the ego must reflect upon itself. But their paths diverge immediately when it becomes necessary to define this ego more closely and distinguish the subject and object of knowledge within the identity of the ego. Unlike Hegel, Kierkegaard does not ask about reality in general; he asks about the reality of a particular something, namely, the reality of the thinking individual's personal existence, the very thing that Hegel ignores. "For all knowledge of reality is possibility; the only reality an existing individual does more than know about is his own, his own being, and this reality constitutes his absolute concern." What is given to the thinking individual as the object of his thinking is his own existence, and he must ask about this particular reality of his own being. He cannot, however, follow Hegel in doing so with the aid of "pure" thinking, divorced from this existence, such as a divine subject might perhaps employ. He can do so only as the empirical subject he is, with the intellectual equipment at his command; he is neither compelled nor permitted to leave the realm of his own existence. His own existence becomes the object that he, the actually existing thinker, must contemplate as subject.

In what sense does this individual's existence become for him a problem that he must solve by his thinking? This problem appears the instant a man ceases to live merely by following his inclinations and drives without question and begins instead to take deliberate account of his being in its particularity. As soon as he does so, he becomes distinct, as this *subject* reflecting upon itself, from his empirical being as *object*. He does not, however, make this distinction "disinterestedly"; he judges the empirical man by the criterion of the ideal man. In thus arriving at an awareness of itself as an existing ego, the ego does not become an ideal ego. Neither, however, does it remain the empirical ego: as an ego concerned for its own existence, it occupies a point midway between the two. But this midpoint is precisely the point at which reality appears: it is present in this concern as an intermediary factor in the literal sense of the Latin *inter-esse.* The increasing awareness on the part of the ego of itself as an existing ego, an awareness that provides the ego with its reality, is the focus of Kierkegaard's existential dialectic. In essence, this is its single theme, repeated with constant variations and developed in every conceivable way. With inexorable stubbornness the ego is held to this point and never allowed to escape in any speculative direction.

Within this existential dialectic, thinking has its own well-defined function among the factors that together constitute existence. The existing, thinking individual, or, as Kierkegaard also calls him, the *subjective thinker,* possesses

> fantasy, emotion, and dialectic in existential inwardness with passion. But first, last, and always passion, for it is impossible to contemplate existence existentially without becoming passionate, because existence is a monstrous contradiction.

The contradiction lies in the fact that one's existence must be that of an idealist—"an exceedingly strenuous calling, because existence itself lodges a protest." To the extent that he fulfills the ideal, a man participates in the infinite, while existence constantly restricts him to the finite. "Only in rare moments can the particular individual as he exists experience a unity of finite and infinite, a unity that transcends existence. This moment is the moment of passion." Kierkegaard finds a striking expression of this passion in the Platonic *eros* of the *Symposium:* "That is the child begotten by the finite and the infinite, which is always striving.

So Socrates thought: therefore love is always striving, that is, the think-ing subject exists."

This does not mean that thought can be isolated from will and feeling: at every stage of the dialectical process all these factors must be present and work together on behalf of idea. At this point, fantasy acquires special significance. It is not a psychically definable faculty like thought, feeling, and will; it is the medium in which these latter operate between ideality and reality. "Fantasy is quite generally the medium of infinita-tion; it is not a faculty like the other faculties; it is, if you like, the faculty *instar omnium*." Fantasy reaches for the infinite and thus also provides the medium for the dialectical *eros*. Kierkegaard can even go so far as to equate fantasy and reflection by defining fantasy as "reflec-tion that makes infinite." Conversely, this association with reflection pro-tects fantasy from losing itself fantastically in boundless speculation. It is directed instead at the particular existential reality that is given as the object of reflection. "How much feeling, knowledge, and will a man has depends ultimately on how much fantasy he has, upon how his feel-ing, knowing, and willing are reflected; in other words, upon fantasy."

Fantasy is more than the medium in which the individual components of the ego become infinite; it is also the medium in which they achieve equilibrium. Feeling, will, and knowledge mutually condition and cor-rect each other.

> Self-reflection leads knowledge astray. By itself it cannot be restrained; the will must also be present. If a man's will goes astray, it is set right by the use of feeling, etc.

But thinking once more predominates, because life is to be "intellec-tually governed." The universal achieved by reflection is to provide the norm of feeling and will. For this to take place, in every moment of one's existence one must reflect upon will and feeling, which set off toward the infinite lying potentially within them as soon as they are set free to move as the eros within them impels them.

But how does this existential dialectic start? Self-reflection linked with fantasy is not yet the movement of existence; it is only the possibility of this movement. The possible self must become the real self, the action considered must become a real action, if the ego is to exist.

If I think, I shall do thus and so, this thinking is not yet an action, and will differ qualitatively from action for all eternity. But it is still a possibility already reflecting the concern of reality and action.

Now there can be no distinction between action conceived and real action; "perhaps there is no difference in content between action conceived and real action; in form, there is an essential difference." Kierkegaard takes care at this point not to commit Hegel's mistake, according to which the empirical ego, assisted by "pure" thinking, is to transform itself into the ideal ego. At this point Kierkegaard instead introduces the will, which transforms the action conceived into a real action. The self takes responsibility for itself by a consciously and responsibly performed act of choice, as we saw at the transition from the aesthetic to the ethical stage. With this choice, the ego chooses itself as an existential ego.

We must not think of this act of choice as a unique event that can be isolated in time. The conscious realization of the ego that takes place at any particular moment is at once taken up in the next moment by reflection and transformed into possibility, to be realized existentially once more. If we examine this act of choice in order to find out how thought is related to existence within it, that is, how action conceived is related to real action, we discover that thought is logically prior to existence, which therefore presupposes thought. But the priority is not temporal. On this point, Kierkegaard says:

> The question of the temporal and logical priority of thought and existence must be answered the same way as the question of directness and indirectness, which Johannes Climacus, in *De omnibus dubitandum*, rejects by referring to the answer Thales is said to have given to a man who asked which came first, day or night: "Night," he said, "was first by a day."

The point is this: with the beginnings of awareness, the ego finds itself in a cycle in which thinking and existing, knowing and willing, converge in existence; this convergence of individual factors in every moment once again confronts the individual in his existence as a new task.

We may now summarize what we have said: It is evident how strongly Kierkegaard is influenced in the development of his own dialectic by his opposition to Hegel. Neither dialectic is concerned with describing a state, but always a movement, a process, a course of events. In both cases the method according to which this movement proceeds counts for every-

thing. Both take the same presuppositions of the philosophy of identity as their point of departure. Even in points of detail the same problems appear in both: the problem of the relationship between thinking
and being, the problem of how the movement begins, and the problem of
the transition from one moment to the next. The solutions given to these
problems, however, are not comparable, because their ways part forever
at one point: Hegel asks abstractly about reality in general, while
Kierkegaard asks concretely about the reality of a specific something,
namely, the reality of the empirical thinking individual. His answer is
not an ontological system, not a system of reality, but the fulfillment,
albeit systematically rigorous in the extreme, of the thinking individual's
existential being.

Philosophical Fragments

Had Kierkegaard lived a hundred years later, that is, in our own day, when a "system" is conceived in rather more modest terms than it was then—when the shadow of Hegel with his all-inclusive system, containing both God and the world, is not so oppressive, when instead the retreat from the macrocosm into the microcosm of the particular ego has actually become the obvious way, not perhaps to construct a universe, but at least a platform from which the universe and its course can be surveyed systematically—had Kierkegaard himself accepted today's more modest claims, he would at once have been able to offer the Hegelian system competition in the form of a system of existential dialectic, which, starting from the existential ego, would have set in motion, with the aid of the thinking of which this ego was capable, a system of philosophic mastering of history that, at least in the dynamism of the movement immanent in the system, would have yielded nothing to that of Hegel. Kierkegaard had already worked out in detail the epistemological presuppositions for such a system in his dispute with the philosophy of the period.

In spite of this, he did not enter into such competition with the Hegelian system. The reasons for his refusal are various. If he had elaborated his introductory work into a system like that imputed to him in our day by existential philosophy and then copied, it would have had to be a system of self-existence (*Dasein*), in contrast to Hegel's system of being (*Sein*). Kierkegaard, however, says often enough that a system of being is possible so long as such a system, like Hegel's, abstracts from the being of the thinking individual himself, but that a system of self-existence is impossible. Why is this?

As we have seen, Kierkegaard takes the field against Hegel within the realm of logic and demonstrates that movement, the process of be-coming, cannot be effected within this realm. This means that all Hegel's dialectic cannot be set in motion. Hegel relegates his entire system to the sphere of abstraction, where self-existence and reality can never ap-pear. This argument, however, is only preliminary. It remains in force, but for Kierkegaard it does not touch upon the crucial point. This prob-lem of becoming, the transition from nonbeing to being, was a matter of deep concern even to Plato and Aristotle. Leaving them aside, Kierke-gaard found far better solutions to this problem in contemporary phi-losophy than in Hegel. They nevertheless could not satisfy him within the concrete limits of the problem as he saw it, ultimately because he came to recognize more and more clearly that the problem of the transi-tion from nonbeing to being is the problem of *sin*. For Hegel, sin was merely a transitory aspect of the dialectical process: weakness, sensuality, deprivation of spirit, etc. In short, sin was something negative that came about because the thinker sought to hold fast to one isolated aspect of the dialectical process, refusing to surrender it to the movement of the dialectic so that, in this dialectic, it could be transcended in positive fashion. For Kierkegaard, however, all this takes on a different appear-ance. We have already heard that Kierkegaard had learned from orthodox dogmatics one of the most crucial doctrines of Christianity: sin is not something negative, a mere deficiency; it possesses posi-tivity. This complicates the problem of becoming, of transition, to an extraordinary degree. Note the concrete form this problem assumes for Kierkegaard: it appears where the self takes responsibility for itself in its natural state, choosing the ego as it actually is to be the ego as it should be. This concern that the ego has for itself results in the move-ment in which, for Kierkegaard, self-being and reality make their appearance. For Kierkegaard, the problem of becoming is concretized in the transition from this ego as it naturally is to the ego ethically re-sponsible for itself. And here the difficulty arises that Hegel and all those that treat the problem within the limits of abstract logic do not encoun-ter—the problem of how to dispose of that which has no being in order that that which has being may appear. What has no being cannot lightly be dismissed as a mere transitional factor; it is present in such a way that one stumbles upon it everywhere. It is not merely the im-perfect, that which has not yet arrived at being in the existential dialectic, in other words, that which has no being in the sense that it does not yet have self-existence. No, that which has no being is present everywhere as a position,

> as the nothing from which creation came, as illusion and deception, as sin, as sensuality divorced from spirit, as tenderness forgotten by the eternal; therefore the task is now to remove it and evoke that which has being.

Now the transition from nonbeing to being is no longer merely an impossibility within the realm of logic; it has ceased completely to be within the realm of human possibility. There is no way for man to overcome sin. The positivity of sin is such that it increases in every moment in which one does not escape from it. As Kierkegaard says, it is "a position that develops out of itself a constantly more imposing continuity." This, then, is the problem of the transition: this continuous positivity of sin must be broken in order that the real self may take on self-existence. Thus for Kierkegaard the problem of becoming is ultimately the problem of the forgiveness of sins.

Could not a system of self-existence be built up on these principles, if not with philosophic methods, then with the methods of dogmatic theology, or with a combination of the two? Not only did Kierkegaard's theological contemporaries, influenced by Hegel, follow this course, it is the course that has been followed by theologians in every period. The trouble is that the forgiveness of sins is not a doctrine but a process, something that takes place between God and man. It is just this event-character that is missing when the forgiveness of sins is turned into a doctrine. But the same holds true for sin, faith, offense, etc., for all the concepts that surround this process of the forgiveness of sins. God's revelation in Jesus Christ is an offense to natural man—and indeed must be, if he is to decide between offense and faith. If this offense is turned into a *doctrine* of offense that can then be embedded in a theological system, then the scandal has in fact been eliminated by being made rationally comprehensible, though only in the form of a *sacrificium intellectus*. The most difficult problem concerns the doctrine of sin. In the Introduction to *The Concept of Dread,* Kierkegaard discusses at great length what branch of knowledge is to study sin—psychology, aesthetics, ethics, metaphysics, or dogmatics. He comes to the astounding conclusion: "Actually sin has no place in any branch of knowledge. It is the subject of preaching, where the individual as an individual speaks to the individual." What is he trying to say here?

We may recall that a revelation from God is necessary if man is to recognize his condition as sin. This means not just a deficiency, but a positive opposition to God. At the same time sin is revealed, however, so is the forgiveness of sin. In other words, this state of sin is declared abolished by God, with the result that man, too, can abolish it through faith. What Kierkegaard is trying to say is that the only form of speech that corresponds to this revelatory event is preaching, which does not *discuss* sin and the possibility of its forgiveness with a man, but tells him to his face, with divine authority, that *he* is a sinner, but also that *his* sin is forgiven, and therefore confronts *him* with the decision between offense and faith. Thus the *event* of revelation corresponds to the *event* of preaching and thus to the *event* of faith, with which a man makes what has been revealed his own. In the passage just quoted, where Kierkegaard describes sin as the subject of preaching, he continues:

> In our time our self-important scholars make the parish clergy out to be fools, whose job is to act as sexton for the professors, whose devotion in turn is to their subject, and who consider preaching beneath their dignity. No wonder, therefore, that preaching is looked upon as a very inferior art. But preaching is the most difficult of all arts, it is the art that Socrates extols: the art of conducting a conversation. Obviously this does not mean that it is necessary for someone in the congregation to reply. Nor would it help constantly to introduce someone as speaker. When Socrates says that the Sophists could speak very well but did not know how to conduct a conversation, his real complaint is this: they had much to say on any subject, but were lacking the factor of assent. Assent, however, is the secret of conversation.

One should add that, important as assent is in Socratic dialogue, it is infinitely more important in preaching, which is concerned with proclaiming the event of revelation.

Now Kierkegaard did not think his own calling was to preach, in order by his preaching to support directly this motif of assent against the philosophers and the theologians whom they had corrupted. He had to do it by indirect communication, by conducting a Socratic dialogue with them through his writings, In particular, he takes on the philosophers and the theologians that were striving for a synthesis between philosophy and Christianity, reason and revelation, in a work that appeared in 1844: *Philosophical Fragments or a Little Philosophy, by Johannes Climacus,* followed in 1846 by *Concluding Unscientific Postscript.* He does not attack directly the synthesis between philosophic thought and the Christian revelation brought about by speculative philosophy, but he betrays his target by a quotation from Shakespeare that he uses as an epigraph for the *Fragments:* "Better well hanged than badly married." The problem to be discussed is introduced on the title page: "Can eternal consciousness have a historical starting point? How can such a starting point be of more than historical interest? Can everlasting salvation be based on knowledge of a historical datum?" In other words, we have here in the form of a question the old thesis that Lessing put to Christianity and Christian theology: "Chance truths of history can never suffice to demonstrate necessary truths of reason."

Kierkegaard's treatment of this problem takes the form of a dialectical experiment. He starts off simply with the general question of whether truth can be taught and, like Socrates, shows that all knowledge is merely recollection. The only function of a teacher, therefore, is to induce the learner to seek the truth within him. This means that, in the last analysis, neither the person of the teacher nor the time and occasion of his teaching have any meaning for the learner and his knowledge of the truth. Now, without mentioning Christianity by name, Kierkegaard introduces a hypothesis: suppose that a specific moment in time acquires crucial significance; how would this affect the question of whether or not truth can be taught? Its consequence for the *teacher* is that he ceases to be merely the occasion for his student's self-knowledge; he must now bring the truth to the student and provide him with the means to understand the truth. But if this is to take place, the teacher must be God himself, or else God himself must become the teacher. The moment in which this takes place must occupy such a special place within the course of history that it could well be called the "fullness of time." The consequence of our hypothesis for the *student* is that his learning turns him into "a man of a different quality or (we may put it so) a *new* man." His learning would show that previously he had lived a lie, while now, since he receives not only the communication of truth but also the means for understanding it, a transformation takes place within him "like the movement from nonbeing to being." This transition can be called *rebirth*.

This thought-experiment is now conducted in detail. A chapter entitled "God as Teacher and Redeemer (A Poetic Experiment)" shows how God decides out of love to become man's teacher. This love remains unrequited, because the two parties, God and man, cannot understand each other. The task of the experimenter is to find a point of contact "where love can make itself understood in truth." To reach this point God can neither draw man up to himself nor show himself to man as God to demand the worship due him; he must come down to man to encounter him in the form of a servant. The learner can be helped only if the teacher fully shares his human lot. But how are the two to reach agreement? This question is discussed in the chapter "The Absolute Paradox (A Metaphysical Caprice)." Once again the point of departure is Socrates, who somewhere confesses that, if he is unable

> to meditate upon the nature of such creatures as Pegasus or the Gorgons, it is because he is not quite clear yet in his own mind whether he (with his knowledge of men) is a monster even more bizarre than Tryphon or a more simple and friendly creature that by nature has something divine about it. This is clearly a paradox.

But this paradox is the supreme passion of thinking: to think something that can no longer be thought. "And a thinker without paradox is like a love without passion: a mediocrity." This unknown that the thinking individual runs up against in his passion we may call God. To do so is only to give him a name, not to prove his existence. "For if God does not exist, there can be no proof that he does not; but if he does, to seek proof that he does is folly." Therefore when we call the unknown God nothing more than a definition is intended. The passion of the intellect dashes itself against this unknown as against its limit, beyond which it can think nothing. Here it comes upon the wholly other, which it can no longer judge because it possesses no appropriate criteria. This encounter brings about a reciprocal "self-ironization of the intellect." Compared to man, God is wholly other; but man can know this only if the knowledge has been vouchsafed by God himself. Otherwise he will continue to think of God in his own terms, which means basically that man himself produces God.

Now when man comes to know this absolute otherness, he discovers that he has offended against it, i.e., that he is in a state of sin. This awareness of sin was what Socrates lacked, what was impossible for him to have. Now if man is instructed by God, the Socratic paradox becomes absolute paradox. This paradox turns out to be absolute: "negatively by bringing to light the absolute otherness of sin, positively by seeking to resolve this absolute otherness in absolute identity." But how can man reach an understanding with this paradox?

> Surely the intellect cannot do it by thinking. The intellect cannot come upon the answer by itself; and if the answer is proclaimed to it, it cannot understand, and notices only that the answer spells its defeat. To this extent, therefore, the intellect has good reason to reject the answer; and yet, in its paradoxical passion, the intellect also seeks its own defeat. Now this defeat of the intellect is also the purpose of the paradox, and so they both agree on this point; but this agreement is present only in the moment of passion.

This clash between the paradox and the passion of the intellect can be disastrous, "the intellect's unrequited love." Then the outcome is not agreement, but an offense to the intellect. The intellect supposes that it discovered this offense by itself, but this is not true.

> If the intellect cannot accomodate the paradox within its head, this is not the discovery of the intellect but of the paradox itself, which was paradoxical enough not to be ashamed of itself and to declare the intellect a dunce and a blockhead, capable at most of saying Yes or No to paradox—none of which yields a good theology. So it is with the offense. All it says about the paradox it learned from the paradox, even when it claims to have made the discovery itself with the help of an auditory hallucination.

But the love of the intellect for the paradox can be rewarded, the intellect can yield and the paradox surrender (*"halb zog sie ihn, halb sank er hin"*). How does this "happy passion" of the intellect come about, this passion that leads to the agreement described, this passion that is called "faith"?

Here I can only sketch the process briefly. Climacus now discusses the problem of the student in detail, stressing particularly the difference between the student who is a contemporary of the teacher and the student at a remove, who must rely on the mediation of the student that is the teacher's contemporary and overcome the historical distance between himself and the teacher. The process of becoming is studied in relationship to what is past and what is yet to come; history is discussed as an interpretation of what is past. Climacus concludes that, with respect to the possibility of faith in the teacher, there is no difference between the two students. As a consequence, the problem of historicity connected with the Christian revelation finds a surprising new solution, which also solves Lessing's problem. The crucial passage in this discussion has gained both fame and notoriety in today's theological debate. It reads:

> If the contemporary generation had left to posterity nothing more than the words, "We have had faith that in such-and-such a year God appeared in the humble form of a servant, lived and taught among us, and then died," it would be more than enough. The contemporary generation has done what was necessary. This brief notice, this historical *nota bene* provides posterity with sufficient occasion (for faith). For all eternity, the most detailed account can do no more for posterity.

In conclusion, Climacus says that he intends to take the problems he has thought through here on the level of pure dialectic and, in a continuation, "introduce them in historical costume."

> But the historical costume in which the next section will introduce the problem is easy to recognize. As is well known, Christianity is the only historical phenomenon that, notwithstanding the limitations of history, in fact with the help of history, has sought to give the individual a point of departure for his knowledge of eternity, has sought to be of more than historical concern to him, has sought to base his salvation upon his relationship to history . . . I nevertheless wished to a certain extent to forget this fact; I used the form of a hypothesis, which allows unlimited freedom, and assumed that the whole thing was only a quaint idea of mine, which, however, I did not want to put down until I had thought it through to the end.

Kierkegaard provided this continuation in the *Concluding Unscientific Postscript,* in whose Introduction Johannes Climacus writes:

Whatever other difficulties there may have been, the problem itself was the real difficulty. The historical costume is easy enough. Without wishing to insult anyone, it is my opinion that not every seminarian would be able to present the problem by itself with the dialectical consistency that appears in this work. It is my opinion that not every seminarian, having read the work, can lay it aside and then present the problem by itself with the dialectical clarity with which it is presented in the work. With regard to the continuation, however, I am convinced (though I am not sure I may not be flattering some people) that every seminarian will be capable of writing it if he is capable of imitating the intrepid dialectical stances and movements.

You will surely be as convinced as I am, and of course as Kierkegaard himself was, that not every seminarian can do this, not even every professor of theology. And my quotation has given you only a faint hint of the "dialectical consistency" and "intrepidity" of the *Philosophical Fragments*. I can only advise you earnestly to read the book itself together with the *Postscript* and not be content with my quotations. I say this for a very special reason. It is not easy to quote from Kierkegaard's other works in such a way as to illustrate not only the bare intellectual outline but also the concomitant "mood." With the *Fragments* it is utterly impossible. I am afraid Kierkegaard would say the same thing about my summary that he said about a contemporary critic of the book:

> The summary is accurate and, on the whole, dialectically reliable; but now comes the hitch: although the summary is accurate, whoever reads only the summary will gain a completely false impression of the book . . . The summary smacks of the lecture room, pure and undisguised. To my mind, this is the most distorted impression that could be given of it. The formal contradiction, the peculiar resistance of the experiment to its content, the artistic impudence (that even reduces Christianity to literary form), the unique attempt that is made to go forward—forward, that is, beyond so-called speculative invention—the unremitting activity of irony, the parody of speculative thought in the design, the satire that lies in the fact that enormous effort is expended, as though something quite extraordinary, something new, were to result, while in fact all that constantly appears is everyday orthodoxy with its proper rigor—none of this comes through at all to the reader of the summary.

And so, since you have allowed a "lecturer," a "professor," a person thoroughly suspect in Kierkegaard's eyes, to introduce you to his work, I must ask you to be aware of the danger involved in such an introduction and to counter it by depending on Kierkegaard himself.

The Borderline
Between Poet and Witness

In carrying out the "Socratic" procedure by which he sought to introduce Christianity into Christendom, Kierkegaard gave literary form to the existential possibilities of the aesthete and the moral philosopher; he did the same thing with the Christian possibility. Of course this does not mean that he was equally concerned with these various possibilities, placing them before the reader for random selection. That this was not his purpose we have already seen through the *Edifying Discourses* that he continued to publish alongside his pseudonymous works, in order to give with the right hand what these latter works gave with the left, that is, in order to communicate directly on a personal level, without interposing the distance required for indirect communication and its irony.

In Kierkegaard's opinion, of course, these *Discourses* were themselves intended only as one part of his program of direct and indirect communication, in which he presents Christianity only as a "poet." He therefore attaches great importance to the statement, repeated time and time again in the Forewords to his *Discourses,* that they are not "sermons," because the author does not have the authority to preach and to be the teacher of someone else. What does this reservation mean? Kierkegaard actually delivered some of these *Discourses* as sermons in church; furthermore, the "Christian" *Discourses,* written toward the end of his life, fulfill all the requirements Kierkegaard made of a "sermon" in contrast to a mere "religious discourse." In spite of this, they are not sermons, for Kierkegaard says:

> A sermon demands a clergyman, and a clergyman is what he is essentially by virtue of his ordination, and ordination is the paradoxical

transformation of a teacher, with all his temporal limitations, which takes him, still with his temporal limitations, and makes him into some-thing different from what his immanent genius, talent, and gifts would develop into.

In other words, because he was not an ordained clergyman, Kierke-gaard can not and will not have his discourses called "sermons." It must be remembered, however, that Kierkegaard had passed the state theological examination and could therefore have been ordained and be-come a clergyman any time he chose.

It appears strange that Kierkegaard should attach such great impor-tance to the precise categorical definition of a sermon with the help of ordination. But let us recall what we learned about Kierkegaard's ef-forts to speak properly of sin and the forgiveness of sins, and how he came to the conclusion that a sermon is the only proper place to speak of these matters. Only here is a man not spoken to *about* his sin, but rather told with authority that he *himself* is a sinner and that the forgiveness of his sins is proclaimed to *him*. A sermon therefore does more than merely communicate the truth: it is an *event* involving God and man that corresponds to the event of revelation. A sermon does not present an argument based on the truth it contains; it addresses the listener with *authority*.

> Authority is a specific quality: it is given to an apostle by his call, to a clergyman by his ordination. The very fact that authority is exercised makes a discourse into a "sermon." This is how a sermon is preached— a fact completely forgotten in our day.

On the basis of this authority, the preacher is not to appeal to the intel-ligence of his listener for the truth of what he says; neither is he to refer to his own faith. He must appeal to the commission given him through his ordination, which demands of him that, by virtue of his office, he confront the listener with the same decision between offense and faith that Christ confronts him with. Therefore the preacher must not allow himself to be drawn into a discussion with the listener about the truth of what he proclaims.

> Christian discourse may have some dealings with doubt—preaching operates solely with the authority of Scripture, the apostles, Christ. It

is therefore rank heresy to deal with doubts in a sermon, even if one should be quite adept at dealing with them.

A preacher who really wants to preach correctly, having read Christ's words to the congregation, must proceed as follows: "These words come from him to whom, by his own statement, all power in heaven and earth is given. Now you, the listener, must consider whether you will bow to this authority or not, whether you will accept and believe these words or not. But if you will not, for God's sake do not accept the words because they are profound or clever or beautiful: to do so would be to criticize God, to mock God!" As soon as the note of authority is struck, this dominant of paradoxical authority, the situation undergoes a qualitative transformation. The assent that was formerly right and proper is now gross insolence.

Now the sermons that Kierkegaard got to hear in the church about him were the exact opposite of all this. In his opinion the clergy usually go wrong in their preaching by not confronting men with the offense, because they do not take as their starting point the Christian imperative: You must believe in the forgiveness of sins. They have forgotten the crucial postulate that the opposite of sin is not virtue, but faith. From the Christian point of view, it may well be correct to say that indifference toward Christ is a form of offense.

> But at a time when Christianity is proclaimed so wretchedly, this statement must be made with certain reservations. There are certainly many thousands that have heard Christianity proclaimed but have never heard anything of this imperative.

The consequence of this preaching is that within Christendom "most men's lives seen in Christian perspective, are so lacking in spirit that they cannot even be called 'sin' in the strict sense." Kierkegaard accuses the clergy of claiming not too much but too little authority in their preaching. "Thus they proclaim Christianity. There was never a word about authority, it was completely avoided. They always avoided saying 'You must,' so as not to incur ridicule."

Now of course there is also a demand made upon the clergyman: his own existence must express what he proclaims. Kierkegaard stresses the importance of ordination so strongly that he can even speak of the "indelible character" it confers. But this must not be understood as meaning that the clergyman is exempted from the demand made on his own existence as a Christian. But this is how Christendom actually understands the matter. The same clergymen that do not dare assert the authority of their office in their preaching instead wrongfully take refuge behind this authority when they are asked about their own existence. It is therefore scarcely possible any more to ask whether a clergyman's life expresses what he preaches. And yet he is

> called to be himself. And in God's house! That is, in an environment (all eyes and ears) that makes just this one demand on him: that he be himself, that he be genuine. To be genuine means simply to be what he proclaims, or at least to strive to be so; or to be frank enough to admit of his own accord that he is not so. Alas, of those that go up into the holy place to proclaim Christianity, how many are even sensitive enough to discover the displeasure and scorn they arouse in the sacred place when they express with enthusiasm, pathos, and tears the very opposite of what their lives express.

Kierkegaard's protest against the existence, or, more accurately, the nonexistence, of the clergy has nothing to do with the usual demand that the clergyman be morally exemplary or "devout" in the pietistic sense. What he protests against is the fact that the clergyman has ceased to be a human ego and therefore does not notice that no real human being can exist in the nonsense that he preaches. Even this, to the extent that it is not merely funny, does turn out to be a moral failing; for the laziness that we have been describing, the frivolousness that is completely devoid of all vocational ethos and is therefore unaware that preaching demands the involvement of the ego, is, in the last analysis, dishonesty.

Kierkegaard does not argue for verification of the authority of proclamation through the personal existence of the clergyman. To do so would have contradicted his completely orthodox understanding of what ordination means. But he does attack the opposite extreme, "for the speaker somehow to cease to be an ego and (as though that were possible) become a thing." If the clergyman's only job is to represent a particular thing, and it is forbidden to go beyond this and ask him about his own existence, then he cannot address anyone else as an existential ego.

> Thus vanished the ego, the "I" that had been the speaker: the speaker is not an "I" but a thing, a point of view. And when the "I" vanished, so of course did the "you": that it is the you who sits there who is

being addressed. Things have even gone so far that speaking to other people in this way is called "getting personal." It is not I, the speaker, that am being spoken of (it is scarcely I that am speaking)—it is a point of view. Whether I practice what I preach is none of your business— if only the point of view is right. It is scarcely my own business, since I owe myself the same consideration I owe others, not to engage in personal remarks. Whether you practice what is preached is none of my business; it is scarcely your own business. It is a point of view, and what matters is at most that you agree with it.

Let us consider the consequences of what has been said for Kierkegaard's own *Discourses,* the consequences, that is, both of his own understanding of what preaching is and of his insight into what passed for "preaching." We do not have to go back a hundred years into the past; it is enough to recall our own experiences. You will probably find that conditions are the same today as they were in Kierkegaard's time. It is said, of course—and the statement is quite orthodox—that one does not go to church on account of the clergyman, that the word of God is proclaimed even by an inferior and unworthy human instrument. True as this may be, a man will be offended by a bad sermon— which is naturally not the same thing as "taking offense" in the Christian sense—or will perhaps sympathize with the clergyman, who obviously does not know what his office demands and therefore fills the pulpit with inappropriate verbiage. With time, however, listening to all this becomes too taxing or too boring or too depressing, and in the end one simply stays away.

Now put yourself in Kierkegaard's place. He feels called to introduce Christianity into this Christendom that has had its fill of preaching. What is he to do? He cannot simply stay away; on the contrary: he should continue to urge men to participate in this worship, although he is well aware what awaits the man who goes to church. Under these circumstances, the obvious thing would have been for Kierkegaard, who had passed his theological examination, to have become an ordained clergyman and preached in the proper way. Kierkegaard considered this possibility time and time again. His failure to follow through seems to be bound up with his personal idiosyncrasies. But the question always confronted him whether these idiosyncrasies did not indicate that he had a special vocation, to which he had to submit. If it was his special calling to introduce Christianity into Christendom, he became more and more clearly aware that he could not perform this task as a clergyman in ecclesiastical office, since this was the very institution that had reduced Christianity to the condition he had to oppose. Kierkegaard never denied that, considered as individuals, there were many honorable and able men among the clergy. But their office as clergy of the state church not only forced them to live in the illusion that all was well with Christendom in its present condition, since that was what gave them their livings; it also forced them to use their office to maintain this illusion.

And so Kierkegaard cannot become a clergyman. In his *Discourses,* without the commission and protection of ecclesiastical office, he must engage in a personal search for the man whom he "can gladly and gratefully call his reader," because this man is more than a mere "reader." In the Foreword to the *Discourses at Friday Communion,* written in 1851, he says:

> A literary activity progressing by stages, which had its beginning with *Either/Or,* here seeks its ultimate resting place at the foot of the altar, where the author, more aware than any of his own personal guilt and imperfection, far from calling himself a witness to the truth, calls himself only a peculiar kind of poet and thinker, who, "lacking authority," had nothing new to bring forward, but rather "wanted to read once more for himself the original text of the circumstances of individual, human existence, the old familiar tradition of our fathers, and if possible interpret it more profoundly."

One must read these discourses for oneself to understand how disquieting it must have been for Christendom that this man not only felt unable to be a clergyman within the existing order of Christendom but even was scrupulously opposed to calling his *Discourses* sermons. This is basically a far more aggressive mode of behavior than all the violent attacks by which Kierkegaard later put the church in tumult and uproar. Of course nobody noticed this, but Kierkegaard himself was well aware of the fact. For example, he gave to his *Christian Discourses,* published in 1848, the subtitle *Thoughts That Attack from Behind—for Edification;* and in the Foreword he wrote:

> Christianity does not need any *defense; defense* does it no service. Christianity attacks. Of all the perversions of Christianity, defending

it is the most irresponsible, the most *perverse,* and the most dangerous: *unconsciously insidious betrayal.* Christianity attacks; within Christendom, it obviously attacks from behind.

Even Kierkegaard's pseudonymous works turned more and more into this kind of attack "from behind." In particular, *Training in Christianity* and *The Sickness unto Death* criticized the present state of Christendom more aggressively than ever. But even here Kierkegaard did not attack directly. He claimed no authority. He described his method in *Training in Christianity:*

> . . . so to unite defense and attack that no one can say directly whether you are attacking or defending, so that the most zealous supporter of a cause and its most bitter opponent can both suppose that they have found an ally—to be nobody, to be absent, an objective something, not a personal individual. If at a particular time faith appears to have vanished from the world, if it is something that should be advertised as missing, then, in order to draw out faith, it might be useful—though I shall not determine whether it can be useful—I shall mention it here only as an example of indirect communication (or of communication in duplicate) —it might be useful to do as follows: represent faith in the strict sense, represent it in such a way that orthodoxy sees in the representation a defense of faith and the freethinker sees an attack, while the communicator is nil, an objective something rather than a human individual—yet perhaps a skillful spy, aided by the communication, might discover the true state of affairs, find out who is the believer, who the freethinker; for this is revealed whenever a person judges the presentation, which is itself neither attack nor defense.

But how could Kierkegaard carry out in practice the procedure he describes here, that is, to write in such a way as "to be nobody, to be absent, an objective something, not a personal individual"? Even if he had published *Training in Christianity* pseudonymously, everyone would still have known who the author was. Pseudonymity could have been understood as an evasion of responsibility. The work could lead to conflict with the existing order, and then his own position with respect to the demand made in the work would have been obvious. Therefore he weighed once more the possibility of taking an office in the church before publishing this work. He might have taken a position teaching in the seminary. In this case his own association with the

98   KIERKEGAARD: AN INTRODUCTION

existing order would show that he could not personally put forward
the claim contained in his writings. No one could confuse him with a
prophet—in his opinion, the worst possible fate that could overtake him.
He writes in his *Journal*, "The effect of this *monumentum aere
perennius* will be strictly in the ideal realm! It is like a judgment, but I
am not the 'judge,' I submit myself to the judgment." But in the end
he refused to take the step fraught with so many difficulties, the assumption of an office in the church. He rejoiced to see that there was
a disinclination to offer him the position in question and that he was
therefore spared the decision. The contrary possibility, however, remained: he might "step directly into the character of the exceptional"
and accept the personal consequences. In so doing, however, he would
have placed too much inward strain upon himself. There was still the
third possibility. He could, as he put it, continue "poetically to
draw everything to myself as a poet, to seek poetic distance in order to
escape any occasion for confusion, as though I were myself existentially
a poet." Even this course was no longer possible, since he had ventured
so far out already. And so, after long deliberation, he found the proper
expedient. He published *Training in Christianity* and *The Sickness
unto Death* under a new pseudonym, Johannes Anti-Climacus, with himself as editor. In contrast to Climacus, the editor of the *Philosophical
Fragments,* who declares that he is not a Christian, Anti-Climacus stands
as a Christian *par excellence*. But Kierkegaard could not claim to be such
a person. Therefore he signed his name only as editor, and inserted before each of the three major divisions of the work a solemnly repeated
"Foreword by the Editor," in which he said:

> In this work, written in the year 1848, the pseudonymous author raises
> the summons to be a Christian to the ultimate pitch of ideality. Never-
> theless, the summons must be given, presented, heard; the Christian
> summons is not subject to negotiation, neither must it be suppressed—
> instead of making allowances and concessions with respect to one's
> own weaknesses. The summons must be heard: and I understand what
> is said here as being said to me alone—not only must I take refuge in
> "grace," I must also take refuge there in such a way as to profit by this
> "grace."

This Foreword was of enormous importance for Kierkegaard's later
conduct. With the "concession" mentioned here, he thought that he

had found the proper expedient, not only for himself but for Christendom. There was nothing Kierkegaard abhorred more than the reform movements in the church that were springing up on all sides at the time. He refused to be associated with them at any price. He wrote in his *Journal:*

> There is scarcely a man as thoroughly initiated as I am into the objections that Christianity can raise to an established church, a national church, the existing order of Christendom, etc. Similarly, I am well aware of the proper Christian demand: separation, that is, the maximum demand of ideality. — But I do say this: to undertake the separation is so much an affair of religion that only a qualitatively superior religious character can carry it out; strictly speaking, what is needed is an apostle, or at least a witness to the truth. And it must be done with character; there is no need for indiscriminate nonsense, without character. To assign this venture to a bewildered head, devoid of character, is infinitely madder than to appoint a streetmonger to command a brigade or to choose an apprentice barber to perform a difficult surgical operation. — Nowhere upon the scene have I discovered a single individual who might even begin to resemble such a superior religious character. There are several, however, that are busy blundering about, undertaking this operation completely without character and in inadmissible form. — This is absolutely pernicious (literally: *corruptio optimi pessima*). The existing order is in a mess—that is not a desirable state of affairs, but it is infinitely preferable to a reform devoid of character. — Herein lies my task. Were I to suggest that I were myself a witness to the truth or the like, I would be irrelevant. For just this reason I am sincere enough to hold in check these immoral reformers, devoid of character. — Thus I safeguard the existing order. — But to do so I demand of it what I demand of myself: concessions. As though a regiment has disobeyed and been stripped of rank: so are we. If it is far from our desire or duty to venture to put an end to this national church and its like, then we must all get used to being stripped of rank and admitting that, in the strict sense, we are not Christians. — This being so, how am I to operate? Do I appear as the man charged by God, so to speak, to strip Christendom of its rank? No, I have no authority. Moved by the ideal, I take pleasure in being stripped of rank myself and striving, "without authority," to bring others to the ideal.

In the Foreword to *Training in Christianity,* Kierkegaard concedes that, confronted with the demands of real Christianity, he can only take refuge in "grace" by utilizing this "grace." This is the confession of his own faith. Now he puts the same question to Christendom: will it make the same concession? Kierkegaard is not only concerned with whether some reader or other will concede the point with regard to himself; he also expects an answer to his question from the official church as the responsible representative of "the existing order of Christendom." Concretely, he expects this answer from the leader of the church, Bishop Mynster of Seeland. He expects the church, through its bishop, "to admit as solemnly as possible that it does not represent New Testament Christianity." He says:

> It is quite simple. In the ecclesiastical realm, the existing order has so cheapened itself, haggled, and sold its services for fear of man that it finds itself no longer in the driver's seat. If it is to regain control, it must make concessions. "A new concession," I hear the existing order say. It thinks more must be conceded to the opposition, as though not enough had been conceded already. Oh, no, no! You leaders must concede to God and Christianity, must do a kind of penance—and behold, in this way you will be restored to power. In this way, control could be established once more over the existing order. But it must all be done with such devout cunning as to challenge the existing order, to see whether it will declare Anti-Climacus officially in opposition, which would force me to express myself more rigorously. God knows, I have considered this course with fear and trembling, even for myself, knowing that the task might be too great for me. But *eh bien,* the die is cast.

It is now up to the existing order whether to understand Kierkegaard's work as an attack or as a defense; for, says Kierkegaard, "dialectically speaking, attack and defense are identical to a shade." Now it is Bishop Mynster's turn to speak.

Attack or Defense?

We must now hear from Mynster, Bishop of Seeland, from whom Kierkegaard awaits the solemn concession that the church has watered down the Christianity of the New Testament, adapting it to the weakness of natural man. It is particularly significant that Kierkegaard casts Bishop Mynster in the role of his antagonist, because Kierkegaard sees in him the best representative of the existing order. Kierkegaard's intention is not to attack particular abuses of the church, but rather the whole attempt to let the protest of the Reformers end once more in the form of a national church living in peace with the world. Therefore he needs a representative of this church who will exhibit as little as possible the symptoms of its decay. From the realm of the "Christian world" he chooses as his opponent the aged bishop, in whom the education and piety of the age had achieved their happiest synthesis. Respect for his father's pastor and his own personal devotion prevent Kierkegaard from attacking Mynster personally. The existing order must be challenged in its strongest position. Rarely have conditions within Christendom for a battle over Christianity been so favorable as in the encounter between Mynster and Kierkegaard. In his *Journal*, Kierkegaard himself describes Mynster's significance for his own work:

> It has been my task to bring about a correction with regard to the existing order, not to introduce something new intended to overthrow or replace the existing order. If I had grasped this from the beginning, and if Mynster had not existed, I would have had to create someone to represent the existing order and would have had to shore him up properly. Since, however, I did not have such a clear vision of my task from the beginning, this point would probably have escaped me; the whole thing would have turned out differently and would perhaps have failed. But

Mynster was there as representative of the existing order. This I had for nothing. It followed quite naturally, since I respected Mynster and did everything possible to express my respect. And so I found my proper stance. Behold, another stroke of good fortune! On the purely personal level, respect for Mynster was a necessity—and so I have gradually come to see that this was of great importance for me, and that I could be set right.

In this way, Kierkegaard ultimately made his own conduct depend completely on that of Bishop Mynster. There were various reasons. First of all, the personal reasons: Kierkegaard feared the conclusions to be drawn from his work—which compelled him to take the offensive —because he thought he was not equal to the task. As always, however, Kierkegaard's personal reasons are bound up inextricably with objective reasons: he is concerned to spare himself; but his fear that he might be forced into the role of a reformer had a firm foundation in objective reality. In *For Self-Examination,* written in 1851, he said:

> And then it shall be said as loudly as possible, and, if possible, heard everywhere, and (God willing!), where it is heard, earnestly considered: *The evil in our time is not the existing order with its many faults; no, the evil in our time is just this evil desire, this lusting after reformation:* this false mania for reformation without willingness to sacrifice; this frivolous idea that a reformation can be carried out without any conception, not to speak of an exalted conception, of how immeasurably exalted the idea of a "reformation" is; this hypocritical failure to recognize one's own incompetence, which busily pursues the amusing idea of reforming the church, a task for which our age is completely unfit.

By linking his own conduct with that of Bishop Mynster, Kierkegaard, acting on these considerations, both personal and objective, makes him responsible for what follows. In 1851, he writes in his *Journal:*

> If I come into conflict with the existing order, it will be solely due to Mynster's blunder. All my efforts are devoted to the defense of the existing order, the only course that can be pursued with sincerity. Everything has been done to make it as easy as possible for Mynster. But if in the end he will insist obdurately that his wretched proclamation of Christianity, which has turned Christianity into an entertainment, is wisdom, is Christianity, then he will be to blame for turning me into something different.

And so it was the existing order's turn to speak; that is, Mynster had to express his position with regard to *Training in Christianity*.

In private, he expresses a negative opinion, which comes to Kierkegaard's ears. In extreme suspense he hastens to see Mynster, but the bishop says nothing of any importance. Kierkegaard waits for a word from him in order to be able to act in one way or another; he waits for years, but Mynster remains stubbornly silent. Events, however, take the course that Kierkegaard foresaw and dreaded, only with the difference that it is not Mynster who commits the "blunder" that forces Kierkegaard to go further, but rather Martensen, Mynster's successor. On January 30, 1854, Mynster dies, without having made the "concession"; and now Martensen does almost the worst thing he can do for Kierkegaard in this situation. In his memorial sermon, he praises the dead bishop as a "witness to the truth":

> Follow in the faith of the true witness! The man whose precious memory fills our hearts directs our thoughts to the whole chain of witnesses to the truth, a chain that extends from the days of the apostles down to our own day . . . In this holy chain of witnesses our departed teacher was a link, serving to the glory of our God and Father. How he exercised among us his witness of faith in demonstrations of the Spirit and of power!

Kierkegaard at once writes an article, "Was Bishop Mynster a 'Witness to the Truth,' One of the Real 'Witnesses to the Truth'?—Is *That* the *Truth?*" In this article we read:

> And so, judged by the criterion of the New Testament, Bishop Mynster's proclamation of Christianity was a wretched proclamation of Christianity, particularly for a witness to the truth. In my opinion, however, this much in him was genuine: he conceded (as I am firmly convinced) before God and before himself that he was by no means a witness to the truth—in my estimation, this concession was truth. — Verily, there is something more contrary to Christianity and the essence of Christianity than any heresy, than any schism, more than all heresies and schisms put together: that is, to play at Christianity. This is what it means—in precisely, precisely the same sense that a child plays soldier—to play at Christianity: to remove the dangers (in the Christian language "witness" and "danger" go together) and substitute force (thus becoming a danger to others), possessions, advantages, volup-

tuous delight in the most luxurious refinements—and to play the game that Bishop Mynster was a witness to the truth, one of the real witnesses to the truth, to play it so terribly seriously that one cannot put an end to the game but continues instead to play it past the very gates of heaven, making Bishop Mynster join the game as a link in the holy chain of witnesses to the truth, a chain that extends from the days of the apostles down to our own day.

Kierkegaard wrote this article on February 1, 1854, but laid it aside for ten months, publishing it for the first time on December 18, 1854, in a newspaper called *The Fatherland*. It concluded with the following words:

As its date indicates, this article has gone unpublished for some time. As long as it remained uncertain who would occupy the episcopal throne of Seeland, I did not think it proper to bring Professor Martensen to make a public statement, since, whether or not he became Bishop, he was at least a candidate for the position and presumably wanted nothing to affect his chances before the matter was decided. When Professor Martensen was nominated, this consideration ceased to obtain. Since, however, the article could not appear immediately and had therefore not appeared immediately, I thought: there is no reason to hurry. Furthermore, Bishop Martensen's nomination occasioned attacks upon him from other quarters and of a quite different kind. I would have been most unwilling to be associated with these attacks. And so I waited, and thought: there is no reason to hurry and nothing to lose by waiting. Possibly something will even turn out to have been gained, possibly a deeper significance will be seen in the fact that the protest came so slowly.

Then, however, he added an intensified summary of the article in order to give as aggressive a form as possible to the public challenge now issued.

There is hardly anything more typical of Kierkegaard's personal attitude than this behavior. Having waited in vain for several years for Mynster's answer—waiting that must have been an unbearable torture to one in his position—now that the decision had been made he could continue to wait for months before speaking out; finally crying out that, instead of the defense that he had offered, Christendom had chosen the attack upon itself. Kierkegaard's endurance of this waiting is a sign that he, the scrupulous melancholic who could never convince himself to take decisive action, was now suddenly completely sure of his course. There is another significant thing. At all other times it had been Kierkegaard's wont to engage in detailed reflections on every point of tactical procedure. The *Journals* of this final period contain almost nothing of this sort; indeed, they contain very few entries dealing directly with the struggle that now claims him completely. All this shows that, unlike his earlier actions, this decisive step was not the result of fundamental considerations. All his scruples and doubts were overcome by that "blunder" made by Martensen, who, quite unaware of what he was doing, could have done nothing better calculated, in this moment of extreme tension, to set the match to the powderkeg. We read in Kierkegaard's *Journal:*

> How it will shine throughout the ages, this memorable epigram on the existing order: that Bishop Mynster should be buried as a witness to the truth, one of the real witnesses to the truth.

Kierkegaard now allows his opponent to force his hand, but obviously this does not mean that he will do so hastily and imprudently. Even now he remains prudent. His ability to wait is a sign of this prudence; so, too, is his ability to relate and yet distinguish personal and objective attack. This is the real criterion that justifies all genuine polemic; there are very few instances in the history of thought in which this test, enormously exacting, has been passed so surely as in the case of Kierkegaard. Now that the stakes were highest, it used concrete examples to show the weakness and dishonesty of Christendom's existing order. With ruthless severity and bitter irony it held the mirror up to Christendom, showing it its own image in a series of typical characters: Ludwig Fromm, *cand. phil.,* who seeks, not the kingdom of heaven, but a state appointment to an incumbency; Juliane, the theologian's wife, who plays such an important role in the procurement of clergy; the Dean and the Provost, with their "ingenuous eyes upon earthly advantage and their speculative eyes upon history"; the young man without any religion who, being a father, must claim the Lutheran-Evangelical religion, which makes a farce of infant baptism; etc. But Kierkegaard is not content with this. Someone must be responsible for this state of affairs; therefore he makes the representatives of Christendom personally answerable and attacks them personally. He does so, however, only when he finds these conditions actually represented by the person. Then he proceeds without regard either for the person under attack or for himself, but taking infinite care not to pick up any allies who are not concerned with the same goal he is.

The newspaper article attacking Martensen has precisely the effect Kierkegaard intended: all Copenhagen is in an uproar. The replies in the press deny him not only all Christian seriousness of purpose and all sense of responsibility, but also all human decency. This impious attack upon the revered deceased can bring only horror to all right-minded people. But Kierkegaard joins battle and conducts it with ever-increasing intensity, first in newspaper articles and then in a series of pamphlets he publishes himself, called "The Instant." In one of these pamphlets, we read:

> This must be said. I oblige no one to act accordingly; I have no authority to do so. But if you have heard it, you have been made responsible and must now act on your own responsibility, however you think you will answer for it before God. One may hear in such a way that he does what I say, another in such a way that he thinks it pleases God, it does God service, to join in the hue and cry raised against me: neither outcome matters to me; what matters is only that it is said. This must be said, so let it be said:
>
> *Whoever you are—whatever your life may otherwise be, my friend— your refusal (if you were formerly accustomed to do so) to attend public worship as it is at present (with its claim to be New Testament Christianity) relieves you forever of one offense, and that a great one: you do not join in calling God a fool by pretending that something is New Testament Christianity when it is not.*

Concretely, Kierkegaard naturally directs his attack primarily against his Protestant environment. It is therefore appropriate to ask whether the Catholic Church might not stand up better before his judgment. He answers this question himself:

> From the standpoint of Christianity, Protestantism is quite simply a fraud, a deception. It falsifies the doctrine of Christianity, the Christian view of the world and of life, when it seeks to be the guiding principle of Christianity and not merely a necessary readjustment (a mere corrective) of specific circumstances, limited in space and time. To enter the Catholic Church on this account would be an overhasty decision, of

which I will not be guilty, even though it might be expected of me, since in these days no one remembers what Christianity is, and even those most self-reliant in matters related to Christianity have little experience. No, a man can be a Christian by himself. And if a man is not strong in spirit, as a Christian he should take the precaution of following this rule: "The fewer the better!" And definitely within "Christendom": "The fewer the better!" For in the last analysis the basic disorder of Christendom, both Catholic and Protestant, lies in the concept of the "church"; or: it lies in the concept of "Christendom."

Even now Kierkegaard's only purpose is to be the "corrective" for the existing order of Christendom. He no longer needs to worry because he lacks the authority to be a "witness to the truth." This is all the result of "providence," which set him on this course and compelled him to follow it step by step. Neither does he have to consider what effect his attack will have, whether it will lead to a proper reformation of the church or merely to a false reform, or whether nothing at all will happen. Since he summons men only to absent themselves from public worship, but not to leave the church, the obvious question has to be raised: what is his conception of a church that corresponds to the Christianity of the New Testament? But he does not discuss this question; he seeks only by every possible means to avoid collecting a group of disciples that might turn him into the leader of a movement or the founder of a sect. It is not his job to give a solution. His job is only to reveal the present state of Christendom in the full depth of its deception. He finds legitimation for his work in the awareness that he is himself sacrificed on behalf of his work by providence. This concept of "providence," which he frequently employs, has a far more profound significance for him than the English word suggests. (See below, page 124.) The outcome of the struggle confirms his faith in his *providentia specialissima*. When he has pushed his argument to the limit and is already beginning to repeat himself, because there is basically nothing more to say, he collapses on the street and is taken to the hospital, where, a few weeks later, on November 11, 1855, he dies. What remained of his money he had used to finance the struggle, and there was just enough left to pay his funeral expenses. The sickness that caused his death remained a riddle to the doctors. For his own part, he had solved the riddle of his life: sure and certain of what he had done as he had never been in his entire life, he died happy, his faith in "providence" confirmed.

Kierkegaard and Posterity*

We did not encounter this enigmatic figure, Søren Kierkegaard, on the streets of Copenhagen, where he involved his contemporaries in Socratic dialogue. We did not experience the excitement and rage occasioned by his scandalously violent attack upon the church. Acquainted with the eighteen volumes of his *Journals,* we know far more about him than his contemporaries did, and so can see behind the scenes. It is not necessary for us to expose ourselves to the purpose of his work as a teacher; we can calmly *discuss* his work and its purpose. We are also in a position to analyze this work into its components, to plunder it like an immensely lucrative storehouse for the scholars of all departments: aestheticians, psychologists, philosophers, and, by no means in last place, even theologians; for Kierkegaard can no longer defend himself against this procedure. Instead of entering into dialectical debate with Kierkegaard's work in its impassioned totality, a debate that demands the venture of one's own existence, the scholar turns existence into the subject matter of a lecture. Philosophers and theologians today rob his work of stones in order to construct a system of "existential thought." But they completely overlook one small but vital distinction: Kierkegaard does not discuss "existential thought"; his concern is for the "thinker with his own existence." This is not the way for posterity to treat the man who has his Johannes Climacus say, "God preserve me from the worst of all deceptions—a disciple."

About the task he sees confronting him he says, "What Christendom has been without is a diagnostician and a dialectician." The *diagnosis* that he offers Christendom can be summed up briefly: Christianity has long

---

* A lecture delivered at the University of Tübingen on the 150th birthday of Søren Kierkegaard; abridged.

since vanished, and yet Christendom lives by it. But now the diagnostician is also a *dialectician*. This means that he does not simply communicate this serious diagnosis directly, which would be to no avail; he does so instead in dialectical fashion. All dialectic can be reduced to one basic form, dialogue, mutual exchange of question and answer in which truth comes to light and carries the day. When Kierkegaard communicates his diagnosis dialectically, his purpose is not to confirm Christendom in this unfortunate state of affairs, but to use the dialogue with his readers to communicate the truth to them, the Christianity they are lacking. *Training in Christianity* is not only the title of one of Kierkegaard's most important writings, it is also the central theme of his entire life's work.

Now the Christian message is not a truth that a man can accept and hold to be true without at the same time laying himself open to the question of how he can exist in this truth, that is, how he can himself become a Christian. But the men confronted by this question live in a Christendom that accepts the obvious convention that all men are Christians. Dialectical communication must therefore shatter this "illusion," taking a hostile stand against the existing order of Christendom.

The man that ventures this dialectical diagnosis of Christendom, which must also contain the cure for Christendom's sickness, is confronted with the knotty question of his *authority* to undertake such a task. Present-day critics of Christendom are wont to dismiss this question casually. Kierkegaard took it very seriously, not only because he was familiar with the difference between a religious genius and a properly commissioned apostle, but also because he accepted the orthodox Lutheran teaching concerning the official authority of the ordained clergyman, although unwilling to become one himself. Neither could he appear before others as a Christian or even a better Christian in order to win them to true Christianity, because he did not consider himself such a person. Therefore he had to engage himself as well in this dialogue. He sometimes expresses this necessity by saying that he prefers to think of himself not as the author of his works, but only as their reader. This is the meaning of Kierkegaard's existential dialectic, or perhaps it would be better to say that this is the *modus procedendi,* the way this dialectic takes place *through* this man and also *within* him, i.e., in his self-reflection.

What is the truth that is to come to light in this dialectic, the truth that brings forth this dialectic and sets it in motion? In his "accountings," Kierkegaard provides two apparently different answers to this question. In the *Postscript* to the *Philosophical Fragments*, he says, "Much labor goes into this work, as though the result were to be something quite remarkable and new, while the continual outcome is ordinary orthodoxy in all its proper rigor." In *The Concept of Dread* and *The Sickness unto Death,* behind all the psychological and anthropological investigations we find once more the orthodox Christian theologian defending the historical contingency of the Christian revelation against the speculative theology of his time, which is connected with late Idealism. To substantiate and interpret his dogmatic position he has recourse to the text of Holy Scripture. In so doing, of course, he does not rely on a dogmatic doctrine of scriptural inspiration, but simply brings the text itself to bear hermeneutically. For instance, *The Concept of Dread* is ultimately nothing but a greatly expanded exegesis of the story of the fall in Genesis 3. In his exegesis, of course, Kierkegaard employs the same independence toward the biblical texts and their self-understanding as he does toward the rest of the literature on which he draws so extensively.

In such statements as these, Kierkegaard traces his existential dialectic theologically back to the revealed truth on which it is based. He can also say, however, that his pseudonyms are "seeking to read once more for themselves the original text of the circumstances of individual, human existence, the old familiar tradition of our fathers, and if possible interpret it more profoundly." Here his dialectic is *philosophical,* basically a dispute with his great antagonist Hegel. For Hegel, truth was found in the universal historical process by which the idea realizes itself and in which the absolute spirit comes to itself, where what is real becomes rational and what is rational becomes real in the movement of pure thought. The Christian revelation once more has a place in this process; indeed, it is ultimately identical with the historical self-realization of the absolute spirit. Hegel could even extract a profound significance from those Christian dogmas the craven theologians of his day no longer dared to defend. The Enlightenment, together with the Kantian critique of reason, had relegated theology to the unverifiable shadow-land of metaphysics, leaving it homeless in the cosmos of the intellect. No wonder theology made enthusiastic use of this magnificent possibility, a synthesis of philosophy and theology, in order to justify and defend Christianity and the existing order of Christendom.

For this very reason, Kierkegaard was forced to turn against Hegel's philosophy in his existential dialectic, just as he was forced to turn against Christendom. He attacked Hegelianism with a single question, to which he returned time and time again like an inquisitor: how is the particular individual to enter into this pure thought? How can a man who is a mere *object* in this universal historical process become a thinking, acting, and existing *subject*? In Kierkegaard's opinion, Hegel had ducked this crucial question, setting the dialectical self-movement of the spirit in motion through a mere trick. To Kierkegaard, Hegel's system was a view of history such as only a god could have, in whom there is knowledge of the ultimate plan to be realized in history, a plan inaccessible to man, who exists within history.

In discussion of Kierkegaard's work the obvious question has been asked: does his attack upon Hegel's logic and his insistence upon its weak point, the transition from thinking to being, do justice to Hegel's magnificent conception? T. W. Adorne, for example, suggests that Kierkegaard misunderstood the concept of "mediation" and its function in Hegel's dialectic and that Kierkegaard's position made him a representative of that "unhappy awareness" which Hegel himself had foreseen and surmounted in *The Phenomenology of the Spirit*. Hegel's interpreters, particularly those of the left, can also object that the transformation of Hegel's idealism into dialectical materialism, predicted by Kierkegaard, was accurately seen, but should be judged positively, rather than negatively, as Kierkegaard did. By retreating into subjectivity, they say, Kierkegaard gave up man's responsibility for history, and his attempt to recover this responsibility by the subterfuge of the "individual" was doomed from the start.

All such judgments are of course determined by their proponents' interpretation of Hegel's work in all its bewildering variety. In any event, one point remains true: Kierkegaard would not have attacked Hegel so passionately if he had had no feeling for the magnificence of Hegel's conception and had not himself been constantly tempted by it. The old observation holds true, however; it is dangerous to let your opponent frame the questions to be debated. One may emerge victorious, but the old principle generally operates: *Victus victori legem dat,* the loser prescribes the law by which the winner must act. Kierkegaard did not succeed in freeing himself from Hegel's influence. In Kierkegaard's work, however, Hegel's dialectic, which encompasses all of world history, becomes internalized, the existential dialectic of the "individual."

But what is the *text* to be interpreted by this dialectic, in whose truth the reader is to be trained? Is it Holy Scripture, i.e., the revealed truth proclaimed by Scripture together with the dogmatic definitions derived by *theology,* or is it "the original text of the circumstances of individual, human existence," which *philosophy* seeks to interpret? We are forced to conclude that Kierkegaard intends to read and interpret both texts at once, without being aware of any contradiction. Therefore Eberhard Grisebach may be right in saying, "In Kierkegaard we probably have the last attempt to combine humanism with the Christian faith." Today we quite rightly suspect all such attempts to construct a synthesis of philosophy and theology, attempts that have been made in every period of Western thought right down to the most recent efforts of theologians to employ existential philosophy as a "formal" foundation, to which theology will give "existential content." All such attempts merely result in a new form of the old apologetics that reduces philosophy to the status of *ancilla theologiae,* to the mutual detriment of both. What Kant once said, with the elegant self-assurance of the philosopher, about philosophy as the "handmaid of theology" remains true today: "It is hard to see whether she is bearing a torch to light her mistress' way or merely holding up her mistress' train." Kierkegaard has nothing in common with these efforts, even though they still frequently appeal to him. He looked upon all forms of apologetics as the ultimate betrayal of Christianity. As early as 1835 he wrote in the first volume of his *Journal:*

> Philosophy and Christianity can never be reconciled; for if I am to hold firmly to the most essential part of Christianity, salvation, it must naturally be extended to the whole man if it is really to mean anything. Or am I to think slightingly of man's moral endowments while finding his understanding intact?

What then does Kierkegaard mean when he says that Christendom needs a "new theory of combat"? Theologians have jumped to the conclusion that he means a new form of apologetics, for which Emil

Brunner has coined the term "eristics." They have also been misled by Kierkegaard's famous (and infamous) statement that he seeks to "trick men into the truth."

All apologetics contains an element of "trickery" when it tries to give the impression of discussing without preconceptions. It does this by meeting the opponent on his own ground and then introducing the Christian point of view *sub rosa.* We are all unpleasantly familiar with this kind of apologetics from the countless bad sermons in which the clergyman enters into imaginary dialogue with the doubts of his hearers—all the more easily since they may not join the discussion—only at the end of the sermon to lapse into emotional appeals that unmask the lack of cogency in the preceding argumentation.

Kierkegaard never let himself be guilty of this kind of "trickery." From the very outset he deliberately published his "edifying" (later, "Christian") discourses alongside his pseudonymous works so that no one could remain in doubt as to his purpose. Even the pseudonymous writings themselves do not keep this purpose concealed. The concluding section of *Either/Or,* called "An Ultimatum," is a sermon on the theme "The Edifying Results of the Thought That We Are Always in the *Wrong* Before God." With regard to the argumentative kind of preaching that is becoming more and more fashionable as the clergy disregard their call to preach, he says:

> Christian discourse may have some dealings with doubt—preaching operates solely with the authority of Scripture, the apostles, Christ. It is therefore rank heresy to deal with doubts in a sermon, even if one should be quite adept at dealing with them.

There must be a clear distinction made between this false *apologetic* and true *apology,* such as 1 Peter 3:15 calls for: "Always be prepared to make a defense [*apologia*] to any one who calls you to account [*logon*] for the hope that is in you." In the case of true apology *all* concerned know from the start *what* hope is being accounted for. Another mark of genuine apology is that in it the Christian gives account of his faith not only to his non-Christian partner but also to himself. This provides the guiding principle that the Christian's argument *ad extra* cannot differ from his argument *ad intra;* if it did, he would be tricking not only his partner, but first and foremost himself.

We must see a transition from true apology to false apologetic when the apologete no longer needs this accounting for himself, but rather supposes that it now lies behind him once and for all and that he is firmly in possession of the truth. It only remains for him therefore to give his accounting *ad extra,* to defend what he possesses by convincing the other fellow of its truth by arguing with him. He will naturally endeavor to leave the defensive and take the offensive as much as possible. But this cannot make up for the basic error of his apologetic. This basic error is for the apologete to think that he can do what the Apostle Paul, for example, could not do, when he wrote to the Corinthians that when he was among them his speech and his preaching were "not in plausible words of wisdom" (1 Cor. 2:4), in order that their faith should not stand in the wisdom of men, but in the power of God. We can also put it this way: what the apologete is seeking to defend and demonstrate as the truth he possesses is no longer that *hope* by which faith lives. It has instead crystallized out as a "Christian" world view, or the like. This makes it something that a man can hang onto securely and with which he can compete more or less successfully in the marketplace of ideas.

We have now arrived at what Kierkegaard calls the "illusion" of the existing order of Christendom. With all its knowledge about Christianity, it has forgotten that the Christian hope is not a demonstrable fact, subject to philosophic discussion, that its truth and validity spring only from a life lived according to it in faith. Therefore Kierkegaard must avoid this false apologetic and return to true apology, which gives accounting for the ground of hope both *ad extra* and *ad intra,* and always with the same means.

Unlike Paul, however, Kierkegaard is not in the position of a missionary to the Gentiles. He must instead introduce Christianity into a Christendom that is already living by this false apologetic. This makes his task of true apology extremely complicated. To his *Christian Discourses* of 1848, Kierkegaard gives the subtitle: *Thoughts That Attack from Behind—for Edification.* And in the Foreword he says:

> Christianity does not need any *defense: defense* does it no service. Christianity attacks. Of all the perversions of Christianity, defending it is the most irresponsible, the most *perverse,* and the most dangerous: *unconsciously insidious betrayal.* Christianity attacks; within Christendom, it obviously attacks from behind.

This "attack from behind" goes as follows: Kierkegaard starts from the assumption that he is not a Christian, thereby indirectly asking the reader whether *he* is one. Nor is this merely a tactical feint, since Kierkegaard really is not sure whether he is a Christian. The result is genuine solidarity with his readers as participants in a dialogue. The claim of Christianity is simply presupposed, without any proof or defense. But for Kierkegaard and his partner in the dialogue, the whole process is merely preparatory to *being* a Christian, not to Christianity. The purpose is neither attack nor defense; or, more precisely, the dialogue can be either or both. Its outcome must determine which it is. Therefore Kierkegaard can say, "dialectically speaking, attack and defense are identical to a shade." He means that his work best defends what is Christian when it causes Christendom to awaken from its illusions and renounce its false apologetic. If Christendom refuses, the defense automatically turns into the most violent kind of attack. Whom then is he trying to "trick into the truth"? Primarily Christians: he would like to help them escape from their illusions and *be* Christians. This category includes Kierkegaard himself. But he feels the same genuine sense of solidarity with all his non-Christian readers, to whom he can say only what he also says to himself; he would like to help them escape from *their* illusions, in which he himself also still lives.

What does this suggest for our inquiry into the relationship between philosophy and Christianity, or the relationship between philosophy and theology? This "attack from behind" automatically prevents Kierkegaard from confronting philosophy and theology in the usual fashion, as personified branches of knowledge. The well-known "conflict of the faculties," which Kant could still draw upon in order to make the best of a bad situation, lies far behind him. Neither does he exhibit the usual schizophrenia, first speaking "as a philosopher," then "as a Christian," finally bringing both into proper relationship. He cannot afford such academic subterfuges. Instead, as a man who has heard the message of the Christian revelation and is seeking to realize its truth in his own existence, he inquires into the circumstances of human existence within which this realization must take place. He is particularly concerned to keep human existence in its unity of willing, feeling, and thinking firmly in view, refusing to isolate any of the individual components and exalt it above the others.

This is particularly true with regard to *thinking*. The modern catchword "existential thought" would have been utter nonsense to Kierkegaard. Having so passionately attacked Hegel's confusion between thinking and being, he knows very well that thinking and existing are two different things, and that thinking always precedes or follows existence. This difference or discrepancy between thinking and existing cannot be transcended by making existence itself the object of thought, that is, by inquiring specifically into the self-existence of the thinking individual rather than into being in general. Heidegger, for instance, was well aware of this fact when he wrote in a note in *Being and Time*:

> In the 19th century, S. Kierkegaard expressly took up the problem of existence as an existential problem and examined it searchingly. The existential problem is so foreign to him, however, that, in regard to ontology, he is completely under the influence of Hegel and of ancient philosophy as seen through Hegel. Therefore his "edifying" works are philosophically more profitable than his theoretical works—with the exception of *The Concept of Dread*.

Heidegger employs Kierkegaard's work therefore almost exclusively as ontic material for the discovery and development of the ontological structures of self-existence. It remained for theologians, following the path that leads from Kierkegaard to Heidegger, to overlook this fundamental difference between Kierkegaard's dialectic of existence and any kind of existential philosophy, and therefore also any kind of existential theology. Kierkegaard's concern is that thinking not be irrelevant to the existence of the thinking individual, that the thinking individual's existence accord with what he thinks, or, to put it another way, that what a man thinks should control his life. It is hardly possible to speak of taking refuge in some sort of mystical or pragmatic irrationalism in the case of a man who sustains the passion of thought in his dialectic to the very point where thought encounters what it can no longer think, a paradox that demonstrates the insufficiency of thought, but nevertheless refuses to take refuge in paradox, or, to put it in terms of dogmatics, rejects *credo quia absurdum* as *refugium ignorantiae*. For Kierkegaard, paradox is anything but an irrational makeshift. He defines it with great precision: "Paradox is not a concession but a category, an ontological designation that expresses the relationship between an existing spirit and eternal truth." He even foresees the abuse to which this concept is liable.

> Paradox is gradually becoming the subject of more and more discussion; before long all this talk, and even *paradoxon* itself, will become *endoxon*. How strange it all is—these people are absolutely free now from the necessity of thinking about anything they say, and are merely eager to get hold of a new word that they can run around with.

Where and how does he achieve a synthesis of what are conventionally called Christianity and humanism, theology and philosophy, or, to use his terms, universal human existence and Christian existence? His answer runs something like this: Dialectic is

> a beneficent force that helps to find out and discover where the absolute object of faith and worship is: it is where the difference between knowing and not knowing vanishes in the absolute worship of ignorance, where objective uncertainty holds back in order to bring forth the passionate certainty of faith, where the conflict between justice and injustice vanishes in the absolute subjection of absolute worship. Dialectic itself does not see the absolute; it leads the individual to the absolute and says, "Here it must be, this much I guarantee; if you worship here, you will be worshiping God." But worship itself is not dialectic.

Of course such a systematization is as easy for the dogmatician as it is for the philosopher. It is quite easy to ask at what point theology and philosophy coincide—thereby doing the very thing Kierkegaard feared that the "pedants" of posterity would do but had no idea how to prevent.

Kierkegaard's *stages,* the ways in which one holds to the categories of life (aesthetic, ethical, religious, and Christian), seem capable in fact of being understood as a kind of *ordo salutis* along which one must pass in order at the end to be a Christian.

I probably contributed to this misunderstanding with my first book about Kierkegaard, written in 1929, *Philosophy and Christianity in S. Kierkegaard,* which presents Kierkegaard's thought as a closed system. These spheres of existence, however, are for Kierkegaard merely the sum total of human possibilities. One must pass through them not to leave them behind, but in order to recover them in faith so as to exist within them in a new way. Such in any case is the goal of all Kierkegaard's work.

Of course this would not be a valid objection to turning this *ordo salutis* into a universal system were it not for the fact that Kierkegaard's own person stands as an objection. At the very place where the pedants look for the point of coincidence, which, like a keystone, could support the whole dialectical structure, there stands a *man*. And not simply *man* as an abstract individual (who does not exist in reality), but this specific man, Søren Kierkegaard, with his singular and in many respects irregular life, which he must work upon with this dialectic of existence. He constantly expresses this fact by saying that he must himself be educated by his work. "Education" is of course far too slight and neutral an expression for what this work does.

Over Kierkegaard's entire life falls the shadow of his father, who brought him while still a youth before the gloomy image of the crucified Lord as the only way to salvation, at the same time laying the burden of his own melancholy upon the shoulders of his son. Kierkegaard not only accepted this burden, he also believed he had to accept the guilt with which his father tortured himself as his own guilt. He clearly had himself in mind when he had the moral philosopher in Part II of *Either/Or* say:

> The greater the freedom, the greater the guilt; it is the blessed mystery of the highest kind of freedom to accept even inherited guilt. Whoever is unwilling to do so is, if not a coward, at least a weakling, if not base, at least not high-minded.

It is in his own dread in the face of life that makes him speak as follows concerning the history of sin in the human race in his superficially dry and pedantic discussion of the problem of original sin in *The Concept of Dread*:

> This increase of dread and sensuality that each subsequent individual has with respect to Adam can of course be a positive or negative quantity in each particular individual. Here there are differences so terrible in reality that certainly no one would dare reflect on them in the deeper sense, i.e., with genuine human sympathy, unless he had previously assured himself with unshakable certainty that the world has never witnessed, nor ever will, such an increase that would transform a quantitative difference into a qualitative difference through a simple transition.

In other words, the burden of the past can never wipe out the future freedom of any man. This unshakable certainty that such a thing cannot happen can come to him only in the message of the gospel, not, of course, in the sense that he *possesses* this certainty once and for all as a truth of dogma, but only in the sense that, contrary to all appearances and contrary to his own experience, he continues to *live,* through faith, according to this truth. Thus he can say, in *The Sickness unto Death,* that this faith is "if you like, a frantic struggle for possibility."

Kierkegaard's refusal to say as much directly and dogmatically lies in the dialectical method of *Training in Christianity.* His own person must vanish behind this dialectic, and therefore he cannot speak as a *confessor.* He is himself engaged in this "frantic struggle for possibility" in order to give meaning to his own life. It is neither possible nor necessary that the reader take a real interest in Kierkegaard's progress, in his singular existence, toward achieving his goal, the freedom of what is universally human. Kierkegaard cannot furnish his readers with a paradigm. In *Stages on Life's Way* Kierkegaard has his pseudonym Quidam say,

". . . in the human sense no one can imitate me." (See above, page 25.)

This excludes all direct following in Kierkegaard's footsteps, all discipleship. The significance of Kierkegaard's work for the reader does not lie in the singularity of his existence. Quite the contrary: what is significant is the way he works out the uniqueness of his life dialectically in universal categories. As Kierkegaard never tires of saying, the exception is the best place to study the rule. In this sense, however, Kierkegaard places the greatest possible demand upon his readers when he has Quidam say:

With all the strength at my command I force myself to hold my life to its proper category. A man can die, I know; a man can die a martyr's death, I know; but a man can hold to his category, can adhere to his category. This is what I myself seek, what I demand of everyone that I admire, of everyone that I even recognize: by day he must think on the category of his life, and dream of it by night.

This brings us to the final question: are these categories worked out by Kierkegaard in existential dialectic really universal? This question is hard to answer in the *philosophical* sense, because philosophy does not

have such universally recognized categories. In this realm Kierkegaard's significance can probably be only that he provides abundant
stimulus for further thought, provided that we are not content simply to
assign him his proper place in the history of philosophy. We cannot avoid
recalling Kierkegaard's harsh words about the pedants of posterity who
will be his heirs. For example, in the Epilogue to his *Philosophy 1955*
Karl Jaspers can say that he has borrowed Kierkegaard's concept of existence. But he goes on to say:

> I have not become a disciple of Kierkegaard. Not only did his Christianity
> fail to move me, I also perceived in his negative decisions (no marriage,
> no ecclesiastical office, no realization in the world, but rather the martyr's
> way of life as being essential to the truth of Christianity) the very op-
> posite of all that I loved, that I was prepared to do and not prepared to
> do. His concept of Christian faith (as being absurd), which his religiosity
> occasioned, seemed to me, like the negative conduct of his life, to repre-
> sent the end of historical Christianity and also the end of any kind of
> philosophic life. All the more remarkable that what Kierkegaard with his
> honesty was able to see and say along his way is an almost inexhaustible
> source of inspiring ideas. Philosophy without Kierkegaard, it seems to me,
> would be impossible today. His greatness—this I recognized—was on a
> par historically with that of Nietzsche.

All that one can say to this is that such hero worship is absolutely fatal
for the work of the "hero." When the existential philosophy that he inspired takes his categories of existence and, unlike Jaspers, reduces them
to a system of "existentialia," we must ask whether this philosophy is
not doing the very thing that Kierkegaard considers impossible and il-
licit, namely, setting up a "system of self-existence," thereby prevent-
ing real existence. The same is true of the various attempts made by
modern *theology* not only to interpret the statements of dogma
existentially with the aid of existential philosophy but even to replace
them with statements of existentialism. It was far from Kierkegaard's
intention to substitute existential dialectic for dogmatics, thereby rob-
bing his dialectic of its very foundation. His objection is to a dogmatics
that claims to be a self-sufficient Christian gnosis when he says:

> A dogmatic system is, from the Christian point of view, a luxury. When
> the weather is fair, when it is possible to guarantee that at least the ma-

jority of men are Christians, there may be time for such a luxury—but when is this condition met? But when the storm rages, then system is an evil, then all theology must serve for edification. System contains an implicit error, suggesting that all is in order, that we are all truly Christians—so now it is time to construct a system.

When he demands that theology be "edifying" instead of displaying systematic perfection, this does not mean (as the word is usually understood today) taking refuge from sober and rigorous thought in religious emotion. It must be understood in the sense that he suggests in the Foreword to *The Sickness unto Death*.

The presentation of what is Christian must show similarity to the statements of a doctor at the sickbed. Even though only the trained doctor may understand them, it must never be forgotten that they are spoken at the sickbed.

And by saying this—once again indirectly—he made a valuable contribution to the work of dogmatic theology.

Here we must ask whether his diagnosis of the existing order of Christendom and its sickness did not also alter the Christian *therapy* itself because he thought that only radical measures would help. Many examples might be given. He can, for example, state the principle, dogmatically quite accurate, that forgiveness of sins must precede conversion in order to make conversion possible. Nevertheless, in his struggle against secularized Protestantism he felt more and more obliged to convert the Reformation doctrine of the relationship between grace and works into a Methodistic austerity. Or consider his doctrine of the *church*. In opposition to a church living in complete harmony with the world, he quite rightly stresses the church's eschatological nature as a mere parenthesis between Christ's ascension and parousia, while within Christendom the church has become an "impatient anticipation of eternity." Or he is quite aware that the *clergyman* owes his authority to his commission to proclaim the gospel and not to his personal piety or moral superiority. But when he sees the clergy abusing their authority and taking refuge in their official status to avoid being questioned about their personal life, and when they fulfill this commission in such a theologically wretched fashion that the Christendom entrusted to their pastoral care learns nothing at all about the crucial facts of Christianity, so that their lives, as he puts it, "are almost too devoid of spirit to be called sinful," then all historical intermediaries between Christ and us, such as church, doctrine, the preaching office, etc., have lost their meaning. All this finally results in the radical demand at which Kierkegaard ultimately arrived: "What is needed is nothing more and nothing less than a revision of Christianity; what is needed is to wipe out 1800 years as though they had never been." One must go beyond the entire history of the church and become Christ's "contemporary." This demand comes within a hair of that extreme limit where each individual Christian must himself become a Christ. When this happens, all Christ's saving work loses its meaning and becomes a mere example to be imitated by each individual Christian. All these consequences seem to have come to the fore in his final great attack upon Christendom; it was therefore all too easy for Christendom to evade the attack.

It would be strange, however, if the great dialectician had not recognized this one-sided radical transformation of Christianity; had this happened, he would have been traitor to his own dialectic. As early as 1849 he describes himself in his *Journal* as a deliberately one-sided "corrective" to the existing order, saying:

> He who would provide the "corrective" must first study in detail the weak points of the existing order—and represent the opposite as one-sidedly as possible; really one-sidedly. This is the very thing that provides the corrective. Herein lies the resignation of the man who must do this. In a sense, the corrective is handed over to the existing order. — If the relationship is right, a presumably shrewd fellow can come along and object that the "corrective" is one-sided—and thereby persuade the crowd to believe that there is something to it. Merciful God! Nothing is easier for him who provides the corrective than presenting the other side. But as soon as he does so, he ceases to be the corrective and becomes the existing order.

Here we find Kierkegaard's idea that he has the right and the authority to proceed as he does because he himself is sacrificed on behalf of his work. This thought continued to grow within him until it became the certainty that allowed him to die happy at the climax of his struggle, knowing that his life was fully in accord with "providence." The word "providence" leaves a bad taste in the mouth, at least for the older ones among us. But that has nothing to do with Kierkegaard. In one of his last journal entries, under the caption "Providentia specialissima," we read:

> To be a Christian means to have faith in a *providentia specialissima,* not *in abstracto,* but *in concreto.* Only he who has this faith *in concreto* is an individuality; everyone else turns out to be a copy related to the type, without courage and without humility, neither tormented nor supported enough to be an individuality.

Which of us will dare to judge whether Kierkegaard, with his reliance in *providentia specialissima,* was right?

"Kierkegaard and posterity" has been our theme. All that I have said on this subject can be summed up most objectively in a few words written by Kierkegaard himself as he discussed posterity in his *Journal:*

> Perhaps it will come to pass, and perhaps it will not, that some person in the next generation will be inspired by your life to pass the examination of his own. His experience will be no different from yours—the examination neither can nor should be prevented; but it will perhaps encourage him in many a moment to think of you, just as you have experienced it with regard to this man or that who is now dead.